Threads of Thoughts
Your Dream's Guideline

Dr. Purnima gupta

BLUEROSE PUBLISHERS
India | U.K.

Copyright © Dr Purnima Gupta 2024

All rights reserved by author. No part of this publication may be reproduced, stored in a retrieval system, or transmitted in any form or by any means, electronic, mechanical, photocopying, recording or otherwise, without the prior permission of the author. Although every precaution has been taken to verify the accuracy of the information contained herein, the publisher assumes no responsibility for any errors or omissions. No liability is assumed for damages that may result from the use of information contained within.

Blue Rose Publishers takes no responsibility for any damages, losses, or liabilities that may arise from the use or misuse of the information, products, or services provided in this publication.

For permissions requests or inquiries regarding this publication, please contact:

BLUEROSE PUBLISHERS
www.BlueRoseONE.com
info@bluerosepublishers.com
+91 8882 898 898
+4407342408967

ISBN: 978-93-6452-823-8

Cover design: Shivani
Typesetting: Sagar

First Edition: August 2024

Acknowledgement

Jai Shree Ganesh

Dhan Guru Nanak

This book is dedicated to **Mata Rani**, who gave me the idea and courage to research and write on dream interpretations which can help a lot of people to find the correct meaning of their dreams. and my **mother Mrs Shashi Gupta** who helped me a lot and encouraged me and motivated me to complete this book.

And all the people who has helped and motivated me and believed in me to write this book and share my knowledge.

(Special acknowledgement to Ms. Jasmine Baweja who suggested me the book title and Canva.com for the lovely graphics)

Contents

Introduction: 1

What are Dreams? 3

Facts About Dreaming 5

Types of Dreams 6

Prepare yourself for dreams 8

Don't remember your dreams? 10

Simple exercise to recall what you saw as a dream while sleeping. 11

Habits which can improve your memory to remember dreams 13

Does Dreams really have a meaning? 14

Different things that one could see in a dream 15

Recurring Dreams 17

Different types of dreams and their meanings 19

Must read before you start interpreting 20

Dreams about Family, friends or Relatives 22

God Or Spiritual Figures in Dreams 33

Animal and Birds 45

Houses and places 52

Dreams about dressing up or being Naked, clothes, makeup and more 65

Dreams about life events 70

Dreams about flowers 79

Travel 82

Flying, Falling, running or attacking and more 85

Health Troubles 94

Examinations 103

Beauty Services	105
Doctor or medical treatments	110
Your actions	114
Sun/ Moon/ Star/ Rainbow	132
Playing Games in your dreams	137
Horror dreams	140
Dreaming about Ex or lover or crush	146
Electronic items	148
Wedding essentials	153
Professions	156
Superhero's, cartoons and dolls or barbie	174
Historic Events	176
Names or Alphabets	179
Other Dreams	181
Dreams about your past birth.	188
Dream catcher	190
Accept My Apology	192
Conclusion	203
Other Best sellers from the author:	204

Introduction:

Dreams are the common part of everyone's life. We see dreams almost every day. It's a different topic that we remember that or no but we see dreams every day. Sometimes we enjoy if we see some happy dreams or some happy moments in our dreams and sometimes, we become scared as we could see a total nightmare and then some forbidden dream.

People immediately have this feeling after waking that will this dream come true? Does the dream I saw had a meaning? Will this be real? Why I am not able to recall what I saw?

Do dreams come true and we think this throughout the day?

This book will help you to discover the meaning and interpretation of your dreams and how and what needs to be done in waking life. It will help you to clear your mind about what you are attracting and what immediate action you need to take to sort your life.

This book is solely the product of my research and experience. I have been interacting with a lot of people and conducting research on their dreams and lives to know how their dreams are affecting them in real life.

What are Dreams?

In simple language "Dream are the picture of videos or simply the experience we feel while we are asleep"

In my opinion: "Dreams are actually the representation of your subconscious mind."

Every day we think about so many random thoughts. Some thoughts we do overthink also and when we focus too much on one thought and get attached with it, we add that thought to our subconscious mind unknowingly.

And dreams are the video projector of our subconscious mind. Everything that we see or feel while we are asleep has a role and significance in our waking life.

It's not wrong to say that when we are awake, we can't know what's there in our subconscious mind and while we are asleep, we could experience it like a movie.

People must have heard about the powerful law of attraction. What we think we attract.

Dreams are the simple way to know what is actually going in our subconscious and when we decode a dream, we get to know what we attract.

Let's understand it with an example:

Take an empty box, every day with random chits and bits of different kind, you are filling that box. Now imagine filling that box for a month. You don't even remember what have you randomly thrown inside. And we can't really open the box and check it.

And the rule says your life events will depend on the chits of this box. Universe has created a way to see what are we attracting by seeing it or feeling it like a video.

Dreams are the visual representation of what we put in the box called our subconscious. And hence we attract it.

Facts About Dreaming

Every day we watch dreams 5-6 times while we are asleep. It's a different topic that we don't remember it. A human mind forgets 95 percent of the dreams that they see.

Each dream last for 5-20 mins.

Dreaming is the brain processing the information strategy and it helps increasing the focus, learning and creating long-term memories.

Visually Impaired people can see more dreams as compared to people who can see in waking life.

Types of Dreams

Dreams are happy or sad or simply the passing of the information that we process in our subconscious mind. Happy dreams can make you smile even in your sleep. Sad dreams can give you anxieties. But is sadness become extreme that can raise your heartbeat too.

And extreme sad or fearful dream is commonly known as **nightmares.** An emotionally disturbed person is more likely to see nightmares. Or if someone who has hold any kind of emotional trauma in their subconscious can see more of night mares and that could be a major hindrance in their healing.

This could be temporary also because of some medication that could affect the hormones or create hallucinations.

There are also **lucid dreams**: where the dreamer is aware in the sleep that they are watching a dream. They often occur in the middle of a regular dream when the sleeping person realizes suddenly that they are dreaming. This could happen either if they have a controlling nature in waking life or they actually want to control some situations given.

Then there are **false awakening dreams** where the person is actually not seeing any dream but is actually hallucinating that they saw a dream which usually comes out of some fears or some excess of stress.

There are **day dreams** as well which people saw during the day if they slept or an hour or two. These are also known as half dreams. As per research we could dream for half an hour during the day. It simply means there are some brain waves that can give you the similar feeling of the deep sleep and your subconscious becomes active. You must have heard people say that day dreams usually come true. It's mainly like some thoughts which are about to manifest and their vibrations are so strong that we could see them even if we are not properly sleeping.

Prepare yourself for dreams

Sometimes, we are going through stressful situations in our waking life and we don't know what is happening and why things are happening in our life. We need clarity of thoughts and mind that what is happening and we need some internal guidance. Dreams are the best way to get the internal clarity or guidance.

When someone wants to see a dream with an intention of knowing what's happening and taking the guidance from the soul. Dreams do come and provide with that guidance.

All a person has to do and prepare themselves for that dream.

Just have a clear issue in your mind before you sleep about which you want to know or take guidance while you are sleeping.

Go to your bed, and before you sleep think about the issue that you are facing and then close your eyes and repeat "I need to know the next step forward or I want to take the guidance for the same"

And then try to sleep.

You will definitely see the dreams related to issue that you are facing and will also see the next step ahead or the correct step to take.

It will be a different story if you are able to recall it or no.

A person sees dreams from a few seconds to 20 -30 mins, 5-6 times and every night. 95 percent of the dream s we usually forget.

But rest 5 percent, some remember the dream very clearly. Some remember in parts and some don't remember at all.

They simply say that I didn't get any dream last night or for past a few days.

But take it like this the brain have to process all the random information you give it or you dump it in your brain. Whenever the brain processes the information, you will see that as a dream.

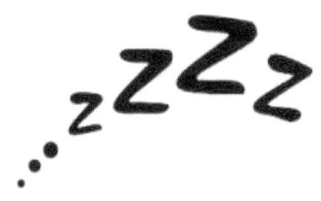

So, dreams you see every night but it's a different fact that you don't remember it. There is a way to remember what you saw as dream.

This exercise needs to be done only in the **morning**, when you are not completely wake up from your sleep or I would say half woke up from your sleep.

When you are getting up from sleep and not completely woke up, at that time your conscious mind is opening and subconscious is shutting down. Dreams are the part of subconscious and we need our open subconscious to recall what we saw as a dream.

When we are half awake and we realise that we don't remember our dream, at that time close your eyes and command your mind that you want to see a repeat telecast of what you saw as a dream.

Command: "I want to see what I saw as a dream last night. Make me see that again"

And your mind will show a small recap of what you saw as a dream. Like a few seconds' long recap.

Things to note: you should do it while on the bed itself before even going to the washroom.

This exercise can help you to recall or give you the similar feeling of the dream you saw.

Habits which can improve your memory to remember dreams

- Keep a note pad and pen near your bed so that you can easily write your dreams as soon as you get up.
- Write small-small details about your dreams
- Any person, stranger, animal that you see.
- Any God or places that you see
- Flowers or water bodies or animals that you see.

Any details regarding the dream are important. The more you remember, the more clarity will go in the interpretation of your dreams.

And when you get this habit of writing the details of your dreams every day. You will remember your dreams faster and clearer.

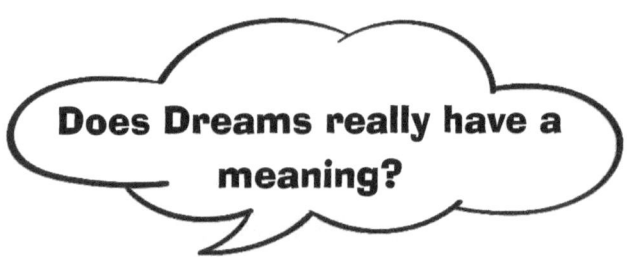

Does Dreams really have a meaning?

Like we say dreams are the reflection of your subconscious mind and as per laws of attraction, what we think or what we have in our subconscious we attract that.

So, dreams do have a meaning and all it requires to be decoded in the correct way.

Dream meanings are not exactly the way you see it. What I mean is suppose you saw a tiger running behind you in your dreams, this doesn't apply that in waking life also a tiger would run behind you or you need to be scared of any tiger coming to your house.

Dreams are in the form of codes, all the things that you see in a dream is not the exact representation or meaning of what you might face or is facing in your real or waking life but it represents something that you need to connect with. That something could be internal like one's personal strength or thought process etc or it could be connected to any of the relations or situations. It could be anything so we need to decode the dream in the proper way.

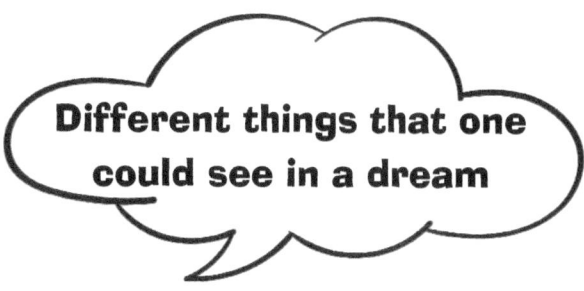

Different things that one could see in a dream

Anyone could practically see anything means anything as you can't really predict how a human mind works but some common dreams are as follows:

1) Dreams about self
2) Dreams about family, relatives and friends or even about enemies
3) Dreams about houses or places, new or old.
4) Dreams about random situations
5) Dreams about animals, birds, insects or other creatures
6) Dreams about flower or some historic monuments
7) Dreams about love and marriage or even of sickness or death.
8) God or spiritual gurus

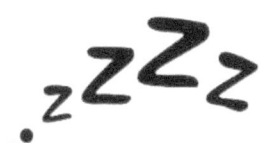

9) Nature and its elements like river, mountains etc
10) Flying, falling, running and walking or sometimes can't even move
11) Dressing up or being naked.
12) Dreams about being late or being attacked by someone.
13) Dreams about pregnancy or child birth or raising a child.
14) Dreams about warnings etc.
15) Being lost or being found.
16) Loosing teeth or some mouth infections.
17) Cartoons
18) Sun, moon and stars.

Etc…

Recurring Dreams

Recurring dreams are in simple language are repeated dreams that one could see again n again. These are exact same dreams or 90 percent similar dreams.

These dreams have a significance in person's life as they are either connected to the past trauma that the person still carries with in or deep inside.

Or these dreams could **come as a warning** that something big is about to happen soon. One should focus on these dreams and try to decode it as soon as possible.

But here the frequency of these dreams matters a lot. Like they should be repeated within a short span of time. May be within 10-20 days max. it should not be like that you saw a similar kind of dream two years ago and you are again seeing this now and you connect it.

Another important thing to notice here is that one should be able to differentiate between similar dream and similar elements in different dreams. Both are different things.

Like for example:

You saw the exact same dream twice in a month that tiger is running behind you in an open land and you are saving yourself from that tiger.

Another dream is that you are talking to a friend and you saw a tiger sitting somewhere at the back. And the earlier dream that tiger is running behind you and you are saving yourself from that tiger.

These are two different dreams but same element tiger in it.

So, we won't consider this as a recurring dream but we will call it as a recurring element of the dream.

Both will have different meaning in the person's life.

Like in first dream you need to interpret it in the exact same way that you are being chased by a tiger

But in second dream you definitely decode the tiger but there is a friend and you are talking to him. That will also be decoded.

Different types of dreams and their meanings

Must read before you start interpreting

Points to note

Dreams doesn't signify as it is in waking life
The person or situations you see in the dream, doesn't implement as exact in waking life. This means if you see marriage in dreams doesn't means you are having a marriage in waking life etc.

If you see a person in your dream doesn't mean you will have something to do with the same person in waking life.

Combined the elements

Like if you see a dream you need to combine all its elements and read the meaning of all the elements separately. And then combine the meaning. To find the exact meaning of your dream.

For egg: you see yourself walking on a cloud and your teeth have fallen down there.

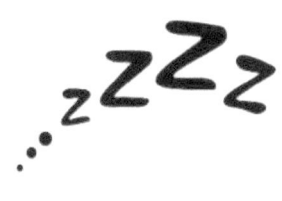

This will involve two dreams walking on clouds + teeth falling.

Check the meaning of both to reach to your final meaning.

Dreams about Family, friends or Relatives

Family (alive or dead)

Father

- **Seeing father falling sick:** this shows anxiety or stress in waking life.
- **Seeing father's death or funeral:** this shows some fear of loss in a waking life. This also shows some kind of unresolved emotional problem in waking life.
- **Seeing already dead father in dreams:** you are insecure about things in waking life and needs some security in your life.
- **Any father figure dies in dream:** in waking life you need to let go of old views or habits and adapt new changes.

- **Father getting married in dreams:** this shows emotional stability and feeling of accomplishment in waking life.
- **Father getting young in dreams:** you need to adapt some old ways of working in your waking life.

Mother

- **Seeing Mother falling sick:** this shows major level of stress or feeling of losing things in waking life.
- **Seeing mother's death or funeral:** this shows some fear of loss in a waking life. This also shows some kind of unresolved emotional problem in waking life. Facing or attracting some major emotional problems.

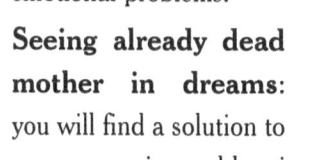

- **Seeing already dead mother in dreams:** you will find a solution to your one major problem in your waking life.
- **Any mother figure dies in dream:** in waking life you need to let go of old views or habits and adapt new changes.
- **Mother getting married in dreams:** this shows the person will gain financial success and properties in their life.
- **Mother getting young in dreams:** you need to adapt some old ways of working in your waking life.

Siblings

Sisters in dreams, shows deep connections in waking life.

Brothers in dream, represents belongingness and family ties.

Happy situations

If you see your **siblings in happy situations** or happy in your dreams: it represents closeness in relationship and great family ties. Any problem related to family can be improved in the coming days. Positive changes can come your way.

Sad situations

If you see your **siblings sad or crying** or in any negative situation in your dreams this shows enmity and feeling of jealousy in waking life.

If there is a **recurring dream about siblings** then one needs to think about their relationship with their siblings in waking life.

If you see **dead siblings** in dreams that means you are losing connections with people in waking life

Grandparents

If any of your grandparents are alive and you see them in dreams

- If they are **showing actions of love and care** or **giving any kind of advice-** it simply means they need your attention in waking life. Maybe they are

suffering from something and they need your help, attention or they are simply missing and wants to bless you.

- If they are **scolding you or not talking to you or angry with you** and not showing any kind of love gestures then they might face some kind of health issues in waking life or they are not very happy with you in waking life.

If any of your grandparents are dead and you see them in your dreams

- If they are showing **actions of love and care** or giving any kind of advice- you will receive a big fortune or good news in waking life.
- If they are **scolding you or not talking to you or angry** with you and not showing any kind of love gestures then you will face some tough situations in waking life and you must be prepared that some problems might come in your life. It could be in any area of your life.

Children

Any children dead or alive, young or old.

Watching your children in dreams could be your daughter or son. Doing anything will bring peace and joy in your waking life. It is  good omen watching your children in dreams. This also means that you will find solutions for some existing problems in your life.

Spouse

Husband

- **If your husband is alive and you see him in dreams:** this is mainly because you are thinking about him or he is the prime focus of your life.
- If he **is upset with you** in your dream: it simply because you might be hiding something from him in waking life.
- If he is **showing love to you** in your dreams it means you are feeling loved in waking life or expecting a lot of love from him in waking life
- If you see him **weak, sick or dead**- he might have a health issue coming up in waking life.
- If you see **your husband cheating on you** in your dreams- then you are getting too insecure about anything in your waking life.
- **Getting married to your husband again** in your dream could mean that you need an old feeling or spark back in your relationship in waking life.

- If you see **doing sex with your husband** in your dreams: this questions the actual relationship with your husband in waking life. Maybe you lack physical intimacy or don't enjoy sex with him that much in waking life.

If your husband is dead and you see him in dreams:

- If he **is smiling and showing affection** of any kind it could be a calming dream and can lead to peace in waking life.
- If he is **upset or angry** with you in your dreams: you are not going happy in your waking life and needs more love and attention.
- **Doing sex with your dead husband**: it simply means you need physical love in waking life.

Wife

- **If your wife is alive and you see her in dreams:** this is mainly because you are thinking about her or she is the prime focus of your life.
- If **she is upset with you** in your dream: it simply because you might be hiding something from her in waking life.
- If she is **showing love to you** in your dreams it means you are feeling loved in waking life or expecting a lot of care from her in waking life

- If you **see her weak, sick or dead**- he might have a health issue coming up in waking life.
- If you see your **wife cheating on you in your dreams**- then you are getting too insecure about anything in your waking life.

- **Getting married to your wife** again in your dream could mean that you need an old feeling or spark back in your relationship in waking life.
- If you see **doing sex with your wife** in your dreams: this questions the actual relationship with your wife in waking life. Maybe you lack physical intimacy or don't enjoy sex with her that much in waking life. This could also mean that you want to have sex with someone else in your waking life.

If your wife is dead and you see her in dreams:
- If she is smiling and showing affection of any kind
- it could be a calming dream and can lead to peace in waking life.
- If she is upset or angry with you in your dreams: you are not going happy in your waking life and needs more love and attention. Or might incur a big loss in your waking life.
- Doing sex with your dead wife: it simply means you need physical love, attention and care in waking life.

Friends

- If you see your friends – **who are alive** in your dreams, could be your best friends and normal friends- this simply means you seek support and companionship in your waking life. You need help and not able to find one in your waking life.
- If you dream about **making the first friend in life,** this means you are subconsciously searching for making new friends in waking life.
- If you dream **about making friends in general** in life, this means you are subconsciously searching for making new friends in waking life.
- If you dream **about losing friendships** in life, this could signify concern for the someone in waking life.
- To see your **dead friends in the dreams**: simply means either you miss them or you need the similar kind of feeling that you felt with a particular friend in your waking life.

Mother-in-law

- **Seeing Mother-in-law falling sick**: this shows major level of stress or feeling of losing things in waking life.

- **Seeing mother-in-law's death or funeral**: this shows some fear of loss in a waking life. This also shows some kind of unresolved emotional problem in waking life.  Facing or attracting some major emotional problems.
- **Seeing already dead mother-in-law in dreams**: you will find a solution to your one major problem in your waking life. She wants you to improve in your life.
- **Mother-in-law getting married in dreams:** this shows the person will gain financial success and properties in their life.
- **Mother-in-law getting young in dreams:** you need to adapt some old ways of working in your waking life.

Father-in-law

- **Seeing father-in-law falling sick**: this shows anxiety or stress in waking life.
- **Seeing father-in-law's death or funeral**: this shows some fear of loss in a waking life. This also shows some kind of unresolved emotional problem in waking life. This could also bring some troubles in spouse's life.
- **Seeing already dead father-in-law in dreams**: you are insecure about things in waking life and needs

some security in your life. Feeling of insecurity could also be there in the spouse as well.
- **Father-in-law getting married in dreams:** this shows emotional stability and feeling of accomplishment in waking life.
- **Father-in-law getting young in dreams:** you need to adapt some old ways of working in your waking life.

Brother-in-law/sister-in-law

if you see your brother-in-law or sister-in-law in your dreams this shows you or your spouse need support in waking life.

Relatives

Maternal relatives

- If you see **maternal relatives**- could be anyone from your mother's side-dead or alive, it simply means most likely either they will visit us or this could indicate some kind of emotional pleasures and happiness in waking life. Some emotional happy news is on its way.
- If you see **maternal cousins**: feeling of happiness and joy and reasons to celebrate you will get in waking life.

Paternal relatives

- If you **see paternal relatives**- could be anyone from your father's side- dead or alive, it simply means that you are  avoiding some kind of responsibilities in your waking life and you need to fulfil that.
- If you see **paternal cousins**: feeling of celebrations along with some responsibilities to fulfil in waking life.

Pets

- If you **see your pet** in your dreams, this shows you crave for loyalty, love and companionship in your waking life.
- If you **see your dead pet** in your dreams, this shows a difficult period in your life where you  don't feel loved anymore in your life.

God Or Spiritual Figures in Dreams

Mainly seeing God or Spiritual figures in your dreams is a result of your imagination, faith and needing for help in waking life.

But their alternate meaning could be:

Hindu God or symbols

Aum- watching the Aum symbol or hearing its sound while sleeping

- **Seeing Aum**- you are getting over confident about something in waking life and you need to step back from certain things.

- **Hearing of Aum sound:** simply means that you are on the right path and you will take or already took the correct decision recently in your life.

Shiva (Lingham or in human form) or Shiv Parivar (Family) in your dreams

- **Shiva-** seeing shiva dancing, happy, enjoying, sitting in calm manner and saying something to you in a calm manner- auspicious days waits for you in waking life. Good days or good news are coming in waking life.

- **Angry shiva in your dreams or doing taandav-** simply goes for misfortunes in your waking life or you are about to receive some punishment in waking life.
- **Shiv with Parvati in dreams:** marriage is on the cards or you are about to receive some good news related to marriage or married life.
- **Shiva with Parvati and children-** child birth or new beginnings in waking life.

Parvati- wife of shiva

- If you see **Parvati alone in happy state** or smiling or advising or dancing- this simply means that you will be about to get married or receive happiness in waking life

- If you see **Parvati with Ganesh or Kartik**- you could conceive or deliver a child soon. Or you could enjoy some new beginnings in life.
- If you see **Parvati angry or in kali Avtar**, it shows some major destruction in coming in your waking life.

Ganesh

- Seeing **Ganesha happy and cheerful** or quiet or eating something in your dreams leads to some good news or success and perfect time in your waking life. These dreams can give you immense achievements in waking life.

- If **Ganesha is sad or angry** in your dreams then you will receive bad news in your waking life.

Karthik

- If you see **Karthik happy or cheerful** in your dreams- you might overcome some biggest challenge in your waking life.
- If you see **Karthik angry or sad** or fighting in your dreams then you might lose some challenge in your waking life.

Maa Laxmi

- If Goddess Laxmi is **happy and sitting with a smile** or near coins or any bag – it simply means you will get some good fortunes or wealth in waking life.
- If Goddess Laxmi comes **in dreams with a lotus**- this dream can bring in good luck in waking life.
- If Goddess Laxmi is **roaming around in the house-** you can by a new property or home in waking life.
- If Goddess Laxmi **is angry or sad** then you will get some financial loss in waking life.

Narayan Or Lord Vishnu

- If you see **Lord Vishnu happy, smiling, sitting** or dancing- you will attract new beginnings and balance in your life.
- If you see lord Vishnu **fighting, angry or sad** in your dreams- you will face extreme situations in waking like. Delays could be a part of your life and you should wait to start anything new in your life.

If you see Ram or Ram Parivar in your dream

This simply means you attract luck and good fortunes and happy family situations in waking life.

Lord Hanuman

if you see lord hanuman in your dream- happy or sad – it simply the blessings that you receive from the universe. This shows you have courage or strength to overcome anything or any problem in waking life.

Lord Brahma

If you see lord brahma in your dream it simply means you will have some new things coming to your life. Positive or negative will totally depend on how you perceive it or how you deal with it but you will attract some new things in waking life.

Lord Sai Baba

If you see lord Sai in your dreams this simply means you are attracting some help for your problems in your waking life. A help will come from the universe.

Lord Krishna

- **Bal Gopal**: if you see a Bal Gopal in your dreams, it simply means you can have a child soon in your life or your children could bring in some good news.
- If you see Krishna **dancing with gopis:** this will bring something to celebrate or happy times in waking life.
- If you see Krishna **sitting on a throne, or happy or laughing** or in happy mood then it can bring in some kind of good news in waking life.
- If you see Krishna **as sad or angry or fighting** then it can bring in some bad news in waking life or your love relationship might face certain issues in waking life.

Spiritual Gurus

If you see any spiritual gurus in dreams- it simply means you need to be inclined towards spiritual practice more in waking life and you are receiving certain kind of blessings as well in waking life

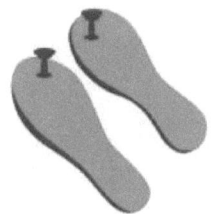

Temples

- If you see **any temple in a dream** but don't see any deities- it simply means you need to understand your inner desires in a better way.
- If you see yourself **going to a temple**- you want answers to some questions in your waking life
- If you see **the temple getting demolished** in dreams: it simply means you will have to face some internal battle in waking life.

Swastik

If you see symbol of Swastik in your dream, it is a good omen and you will receive blessings of the universe in waking life.

Religious products like shank or bell or Deepak etc

If you see any spiritual product in dreams that means it's your spiritual calling and you need to perform some spiritual activities in waking life.

Hawan

If you see hawan happening in your dreams- it simply means you need to leave any bad habit in your waking life.

Sikh Religion

Guru Nanak dev ji

If you see Guru Nanak dev ji in your dreams it simply means you are about to receive some awareness about a situation in your waking life that can lead you towards positivity.

Gurus other than Guru Nanak ji

If you see any Other Sikh Gurus other than Guru Nanak ji then you are attracting great and deep knowledge, success in competitive exams and excel in your studies.

Gurudwara

If you see a gurudwara in your dreams then it simply means that you need to do or focus on charity in waking life or in simple language it means to do Sewa in the waking life.

Muslim religion

Allah

If you see Allah in your dreams this simply means all your sins are forgiven and you are karmic debt free in life.

Mosque

If you see a mosque in your dream- it simply a reminder to do good for people in waking life.

If you see going to Hajj- it simply means there is a spiritual awakening in waking life and you are about to find answers for your problems in waking life.

Christianity

Jesus

If you see Jesus in your dreams, it simply brings comfort and reassurance during challenge if you are facing any in real life, and also signifying divine intervention and offering healing and hope.

Mother Marry:

If you see Mother Mary in your dreams it simply means you are attracting some love, care and attention in waking life and also you can conceive or deliver a baby soon if you are planning that one. It's an ultimate blessing to receive love from the universe.

Church

Seeing a church in your dreams simply means you need some guidance or support in waking life. there could be a conflict that you face within and you need answers for that.

Christmas Tree

Seeing a Christmas tree in your dreams is a good omen. This signifies being happy and celebrations in waking life. In short, all things positive in waking life.

Cross

If you see a cross in dreams simply adds healing to your waking life.

Others

Religious Books

It could be of any religion- it simply means you need to learn a lot of things in waking life. This can go for some courses or higher education in waking life.

Changing your religion

If you see changing your religion in your dreams is simply means you need to change the way, how you deal with the problem in waking life. You need to adapt some new ways to deal with your situations in waking life.

Angels

If you see angels in your dream, it's a good omen. This shows healing, comfort and success in your waking life.

Feathers

- If you see **feather lying on the road,** it is a good omen and you will be receiving blessings from the universe.
- If you see a feather **falling from sky**, it shows your life problems will be solved soon.

Devil/Monsters

If you see a devil in dreams, it's a bad omen and you might receive bad news in your waking life.

Animal and Birds

Ants

If you see ants in your dreams, it simple means you are feeling irritated with someone in waking life.

Bull

If you see a bull in dreams, it shows that you getting aggressive in waking life and you need to control your anger or expectations in your waking life.

Cats

If you see a cat in your dreams, this shows your feminine side, softness and independent spirit in waking life.

Cows

If you see cow in dreams, it means you need to be more aware about what you want in waking life emotionally. This is a warning that you are taking a wrong decision about your emotions in waking life and you need to analyse your decisions.

Crocodiles, alligators or reptiles

- If you these **reptiles i**n your dreams, it simply means you are manifesting your subconscious. Positive or negative that time will tell but you are in manifesting phase and you will soon be converting your thoughts to reality.

- If you see a crocodile **attacking you**, it simply means you are attracting good luck and success in waking life.

Dangerous animals like Hyna, coyotes, leopards

You need to protect yourself from people in waking life. This shows some kind of betrayal coming your way because of some people.

Dinosaurs

- If you see a **dinosaur in your dream**, it symbolises your past or your past memories.
- If you see yourself **riding on a dinosaur**, this shows you are able to process the pain of your past life and moving ahead from your past.
- If you see a dinosaur **attacking you in your dream**, means your past still haunts you and you are not able to move ahead from your past memories.

Dogs

If you see dogs in your dreams its simply shows your faithfulness to your relationships in waking life.

Donkey and Ox

If you see donkey or ox in dreams, simply means you are burdened with responsibilities in waking life.

Elephants

If you see elephants in your dreams, it simply means your emotions are overpowering you in waking life. You need to have a practical approach in dealing with issues in your waking life.

Fishes

- If you **see fishes in your dreams**, this shows you are in good position in waking life and soon you will have materialist gain in waking life.

- If you see yourself **playing with fishes** in your dream, this shows you are exploring a materialistic opportunity in your waking life.

- If you see a **giant fish is attacking you in** your dream, this shows you feel threatened to lose your possessions or might be having some emotional trouble.

Goats, sheep, dear and lamb

If you see any of the above animal in the dream, it simply means you are too lazy about your situation and keeps on avoiding things in waking life. You need to be more serious and active in handling things.

Horse

If you see a horse in dreams, it means you want to win a certain situation in your waking life. This could also mean that this is the time to leave things on the universe and let time unfolds it.

Insects

- If you see an insect in your dreams, this could mean a feeling of guilt or anxiety in waking life.
- If you see **an insect biting you** in your dreams, this means lack of communication between your conscious and subconscious mind.

Monkeys and Apes

If you see a lot of monkeys and apes in dreams simply means you need to improve your social behaviours and need to be more active with people in your waking life.

Owl

If you see an owl in your dream, this is a bad omen and you might receive bad news very soon in waking life

Peacock

Seeing a peacock in your dreams is a good omen. It shows new birth, new life and rejuvenation. It shows positive new beginnings.

Parrot

If you see a parrot in your dream, it simply means you are repeating things in your life and you need to find new way to deal with your stuff rather than following the same old idea or way.

Pigeons

If you see pigeons in your dreams this simply shows that you need a break from life or from your hectic routine and enjoy your life a bit. It's a very fortunate dream and some consider this as a blessing.

Pigs

If you see pigs in your dreams, it simply shows some excitement or enjoyment moments in waking life.

Rats or mice

If you see rats or dirty rats in your dreams, simply means you need to focus on cleanliness in your waking life.

Rabbits and squirrels

If you see any of these animals in dreams, simply means you are running too fast in waking life and you need to slow down in waking life.

Snakes

- If you see **one large and big snake** like anaconda in your dreams that means you are attracting healing and transformation in waking life
- If you see **small snakes** in your dreams which simply means you are attracting some betrayal or deceit or some hidden threats in your waking life.
- If you see many snakes **together sitting or chasing you-** it simply means you might have some health issues in waking life.
- If snake is **eating you in your dream**- it simply means you need to have courage and strength for the problem you are facing in waking life.

Tiger

Tiger in your dream symbolises inner strength, power and courage. You have it in you whatever is the problem that you are facing in waking life, you have the power and strength inside you to overcome it

- If you see a **tiger is attacking you or chasing you**- it simply a reminder that you are running away from some problem or feeling unnecessary weak in waking life but you have the power and courage in you.

Turtle/Tortoise

If you see a turtle in your dream this shows there is a need for patience in your situations in waking life.

Any other bird

Birds are generally the symbol of good luck and prosperity and can bring in a lot of success in waking life.

Houses and places

Airports

- If you see yourself at the **airport or outside** the airport in your dreams, it simply means new beginnings are coming in your waking life.
- If you see **yourself boarding a flight or in a flight** in your dream, it simply means you are about to start a new chapter or phase of your life and it will be positive.

Bridge

- If you see yourself **crossing the bridge**, it means that you want to renew any old friendships in your waking life or you need to fill the gap in your relationships in waking life.
- If you see yourself **standing on the bridge** or walking on the bridge in your dreams that means you want to improve your communication with someone in your waking life.

- If you see a **bridge falling or collapsed** in your dreams that simply means you passed an opportunity and it might not come back.

Basement in dreams

- If you see a **basement in dreams from far way** that means you fear something in waking life and you need to address that fear as soon as possible.
- If you **feel stuck in basement** in your dreams – it simply means your fears in life has taken over your mind and you feel trapped or going through anxiety in your waking life.

Bus stand

- If you see **yourself at Bus stand** in your dreams that means you are facing a crossroads in your waking life.
- If you see yourself **boarding a bus** and sitting in a bus in a dream, it simply means you feel stuck in waking life and have a desire to move on.

Clubs or Bars

If you see having party at the club in your dreams, it simply means you might incur some issues in careers.

Caves

- If you see **walking or passing through a cave** in your dreams, means there is a good chance you are exploring your own potential and ready for personal evolution.
- If you **feel stuck in a cave in your dream**, it means you are stuck to some personal habit in your life.

Courts or lawyer chambers

- If you see yourself **visiting a court** and inside the court room in dreams, it simply means you are looking for justice in your waking life.
- If you see **yourself talking to a lawyer** in the court or lawyer chambers in your dreams, it simply means that you want to be heard and listen to in your waking life.

Car Parking/any other vehicle

- If you see yourself **parking your car** in your dreams, this shows that you control the direction where you are heading in life.
- If you **see others parking the car** in your dreams, you are actually evaluating the opportunities that others got in your life.

- If you see **someone is towing your car** in your dreams, this means someone is taking away the opportunity which is meant for you in your waking life.
- If you see **a car parked in car parking** your dream, this shows that you're re-evaluating your resources available in life.

Cremation ground or cemetery

If you see a cemetery or cremation ground in your dreams or any dreams related to that it means some major health issues are coming in waking life.

Foreign country

- If you see yourself living or **settling in a foreign country**, it simply means you feel unsettled in your waking life.
- If you see **visiting a foreign country for temporary basis**, it simply means you need a break from your routine in waking life and you crave for some changes in your waking life.

Fridge or cold storage

- If you see an **open fridge or cold storage** in the dreams, it means you are searching for something in waking life. You could be desperate about somethings and you want it.
- If you see that **you are trapped in a fridge or cold storage** in your dreams, it means you are getting highly disappointed with your desires.

Houses

- **Dream House:** that you always dream about but don't own- if you dream about your dream houses it simply means that you subconscious is trying to warn you about your inner desires and soul wishes. You should concentrate more on what you really want in life rather than running behind immaterial things.

- **House where you live- if you see a house where you live currently,** this simply means you need to focus on the necessities in waking life. Like what is required rather than what you desire.

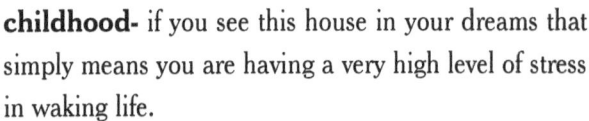

- **House where you live previously or in your childhood-** if you see this house in your dreams that simply means you are having a very high level of stress in waking life.

- **Demolished house-** if you see a demolished house in dreams that simply means your plans in waking life won't be successful and you might have to change the way you think or act in a certain way.

- **Under construction houses in dreams-** if you see a house getting constructed in the dreams that simply means your plans and ideas are takings its shape and soon you will be able to get the solution for what you need the most in your life.

- If you see yourself **buying a house in dreams**, it shows your desire for security in waking life. You want to secure yourself from all ends.
- **Locked house-** if you see any house that is locked and you are not able to enter inside the house- this simply means you have taken a wrong decision in your life recently and you need to rethink about your decisions in waking life.

Hotels

- If your see yourself checking in or **staying in a hotel** in your dreams, it means you are moving from one phase to another in your career or relationship in your waking life.
- If your see yourself **checking out from your hotel** in your dreams, it means you need to analyse your career and relationship in waking life.

Hospitals

- If you see yourself **at the hospital** or visiting a hospital in your dreams, it means you are afraid about some kind of health issues in waking life.
- If you see yourself **getting a treatment** done in the hospital or clinic in your dreams, it means you are going through a period of change or renewal in waking life.
- If you **take others to the hospital** for treatment in your dreams it simply means that you are looking for a help in your waking life.

Market

- If you see **markets in your dreams**, it shows your desires to socialise with others, maybe you want to make new friends.
- If you see yourself **shopping in the market**, it shows that you want to celebrate something with people or your social circle in waking life.
- If you see that **you don't have the money** to buy anything in market in your dreams, it means that you are very lonely in your waking life or shows some kind of misunderstanding in your relationships in waking life.

Mountains

- If you see **yourself climbing a mountain** in your dreams, it means that you are about to overcome a challenge in your waking life.
- If you see yourself at the **peak of the mountain** in your dreams, it means that you won a big battle in your waking life. Life was not easy but you have made it.
- If you see yourself **falling from the mountain** in your dreams, it means you are feeling out of control in some situation in waking life.

Museum

If you see yourself visiting a museum in dreams, this shows you are thinking about your past events a lot in waking life which might affect your future.

Office or commercial buildings or spaces in dreams-

It simply shows your career aspirations and that you are becoming over ambitious in life. you need to control taking any kind of career decisions recently in waking life.

Open Land

If you see an open land in your dreams, it simply a symbol of wealth and you might gain wealth in your life.

Parks-

If you see a park in your dreams or see yourself walking, running or visiting a park- this simply means follow your emotions in waking life rather than your mind and you will be internally happy.

Play ground

- If you see yourself **standing or sitting** in a playground in your dreams, it simply means that you want to enjoy in waking life but something is blocking that and you aren't able to fully enjoy your life.
- If you see **yourself playing in a playground** in your dreams, it simply means that you are happy in waking life and enjoying it fully.

Police station or jail

- If you see a police station **or visiting a** police station or jail in your dreams, it simply means that you need a guidance to resolve your issues in waking life. You need to speak to someone who can provide you the best possible guidance.
- If you **see yourself locked up in jail** in your dreams, it simply means you will attract one major problem (could be related to anything) in your waking life.
- If you see yourself getting **an FIR done** or someone has registered an FIR against you, it simply means you need to be careful about all the paperwork in your waking life.
- If someone **is beating you** in police station in dreams it means you will attract some health issues in waking life.

Places that you haven't ever visited in real life

If you find yourself dreaming about the places which you haven't ever visited in waking life, it simply means you want to escape from the situations in waking life and you need to need to find peace by visiting some spiritual place.

Restaurant or café's

- If you see **yourself going to a café** or restaurant it signifies a desire for nourishment, both physically and emotionally.

- If you see yourself **eating alone in a restaurant** in your dream- it means that you are lonely in your waking life.
- If you see yourself **eating with people in restaurant** or café in your dreams, it means that you need to make specific changes in your life for a healthy body and relationships.
- If you see yourself **washing dishes in a café or restaurant** in your dream it means you will get bad news in your waking life.
- If you **don't have the money to pay the bill** at the café or restaurant in your dream it simply means you will face some financial loss in your waking life.

Railway station

- If you see yourself **at the railway station or platform** in your dreams, it simply means that a transformation is about to come in your waking life. It could be slow but would prove to be a positive one.
- If you see yourself **in a train or boarding a train** or sitting in a train in dreams, it simply means that you

are excited about something in your waking life that could be a change or a new thing that is about to begin.

Sea or river or lakes or oceans

- If you see a **sea/river/ lake shore** in your dreams- it simply means you are going through or soon encounter some emotional issues in life
- If you see **waves in sea/oceans** in your dreams, it simply means you are going through some emotional troubles or anxieties in your waking life.
- If you see **falling into sea/river/ lake/oceans** in your dreams that simply is a sign of panic attacks and emotional troubles in waking life.
- If you see **yourself on a boat or ship** and in the middle or shore of the sea or any water body, it simply means that soon you will find a help for your emotional troubles in waking life.

- **Swimming in any water body** in dreams means that you have the courage and strength to face any life challenge that is coming your way.
- If you see **yourself drinking sea water**- it simply means you are absorbing emotional pain in waking life.
- If you see **yourself swimming in a swimming pool,** this is the time cleanse your life problems especially emotional ones.

Spiritual places

- If you see yourself going to spiritual places- you want answers to some questions in your waking life.

Schools and College

- If you see yourself **in school, college** or in any educational institute in your dreams, this shows you need to move forward in life and learn some new skills.
- If you see yourself **going to a new school or college** or any other educational institute in your dreams, it means some embarrassing situations in waking life.
- If you see yourself **returning to school** after long in your dreams, it means you got a negative effect from some situations in waking life but you realised it later.

Stairs

- If you **are walking up the stairs** in your dreams, it simply means you have faced something very disappointing in your life from which you need to move on in your waking life.
- If you see **walking down the stairs** in your dreams, it means there will be something in waking life to look forward too.

Theatres or picture hall

If you see yourself in theatres or picture halls – sitting or watching a play or movie, it means a truth is about to be revealed in waking life

Village

- If you see **yourself going or visiting a village** in your dreams, this shows following some traditional approach in waking life.
- If you see yourself **thrown out of the village,** this shows that you don't follow traditional ways and very liberal or modern in your approach.
- If you see yourself **working in a village**, this shows that you are trying to maintain a balance between your traditions and modern world.

Zoo

If you see or visit a zoo in your dreams it means you are feeling trapped or not able to feel free in waking life.

Naked dreams

- If you see **yourself partially naked** (you don't have your top on) in your dreams, it simply means you have just something off your chest- could be a guilt or emotional troubles or anything else but you feel lighter in your waking life.

- If you see **yourself partially naked** (you don't have your bottom on) in your dreams, this means you feel vulnerable in waking life and sometimes this dream could come as a result of sex cravings.

- If you see **yourself completely naked** in your dreams, it means you are scared that your secret could be out and you won't be able to hide it from people.

- If you see any **other person naked** in the dream partial or complete, and that person is **close to you**, it means they are trying to open to you about their situations, maybe they need any help or they just want to talk.

- If you see **any other person** naked in the dream partial or complete, and that person is a **complete stranger**, this means that you are facing an embarrassing situation in real life and trying to hide yourself from the world.

Dressing up

- If you are **getting ready or dressed** up in your dreams, it means you are very much satisfied with yourself and you appreciate yourself in waking life.

- If you are **dressed up like someone** in dreams- it means you need to adapt their qualities in waking life.
- If you **undress yourself in dreams,** it means you are not satisfied with something in waking life and you want to change it.
- If **someone else is getting dressed up or undress** in front of you in your dreams, it means you are getting attracted towards someone in waking life or this could resemble sexual desires.

Make up

- If you see yourself **doing makeup** or with makeup in your dream, it means you are hiding things from someone in waking life or you are not able to express yourself completely.
- If you see yourself **removing makeup** in your dreams, it means either you are about to make any confessions in your waking life or you will express yourself to people in a better way in waking life.

- If you see **someone else doing the makeup** in your dreams, it means other people are hiding something from you in waking life.
- If you see yourself **throwing away makeup** items in your dreams, it means you are tired of hiding things in waking life and you want to be honest and face the realities in waking life.

Clothes

- If you see yourself **buying dresses** or clothes (other than wedding dress) in your dreams, it means you want to start a fresh in waking life. Some new beginning you want in waking life.
- If you see yourself **buying a wedding dress** for yourself in your dreams, it means you are ready for real commitment and relationship in waking life.

- If you see **yourself buying a wedding dress for someone else** in your dreams, it simply means you are happy for someone in waking life. It could be for any achievement that they made in waking life.
- If you see **yourself donating clothes** to someone in your dreams, it means you are very well aware of your strength and weakness and you could be exploiting your strengths in waking life.
- If you see **yourself stitching clothes** for people in your dreams, it means you are hiding secrets of others in your heart or mind in waking life.

Shoes or sandals (any type of footwear)

- If you see **yourself wearing shoes/ sandals** in dreams, this represents your connection between soul and body in waking life. You are awake about your soul's desires, that what you really want.
- If you see yourself **buying shoes** in your dreams, it means a transformation is about to take place in you waking life where you will be aware about your inner desires.
- If you see yourself **donating shoes** to someone in your dreams, it means you are sacrificing some of your desires for people in waking life.
- If you see **yourself making shoes** in your dreams, it means you are building your character in waking life.

Accessories

- If you see yourself **wearing accessories** like jewellery watches or bags in your dreams – it means you value yourself in waking life. The power of selflove is within love and you enjoy your own company.

- If you see **giving up your jewellery or accessories** to someone in your dream, it means someone is not valuing you enough in waking life or you might have to face some insult in waking life.

Dreams about life events

If you see any life event in dreams, that doesn't mean that life event is coming into your life but it simply means the following:

Child Birth

- If you see that you are **getting pregnant** or you are pregnant in your dream, it means you need to analyse your life, something is in growing phase. This could be an idea, a relationship or a problem etc.
- If you **see delivering a child** in your dreams, this simply means change in emotions or emotional rebirth in waking life.

- If you see your **own miscarriage** in your dreams, this means either you are having anxiety issues or have fear about something.

- If you see **someone else is getting pregnant** in your dreams, this simply means you are enjoying some new friendships in your waking life.
- If you see **someone else's miscarriage** in your dreams, it means you are not able to fully trust someone or is scared of someone in your waking life.
- If you dream about **when your child has spoken or is speaking the first words**, this simply means you are taking baby steps towards something in real life.

Death

- If you see your **own dead body** or death in your dream, it means closing a chapter of your life and that closing could be painful. It could be a job or relationship or anything else but something is about to end in your life.
- If you **see your body getting cremated** or buried in dream, it means you are out of some old trauma and pain and entering a new phase in your waking life.
- If you see **death of someone else** other than your partner in your dream, it means one of your relationships is about to get over in waking life.
- If you see death **or dead body of your partner**, it means this could be an indication that they are changing in some or the other way.

Divorce

- If you see yourself **getting divorced** in your dreams, it simply means that you fear of losing a loved one not necessarily your partner, in your waking life.
- If you see **someone else getting divorced** in dreams, it means that you have a fear of losing people in your waking life.
- If you see you are **fighting for divorce case** in court in your dreams, it could show you current situations, or you might be falling into a trap in waking life.
- If you are thinking in your dreams that you **want to take divorce from your partner,** this shows trust issues in waking life. You aren't able to trust people that easily in waking life.

Engagement or Roka

- If you see **getting engaged to someone known** in dreams, it means you are about to make a deeper commitment to a person, job or situation in waking life.
- If you see **getting engaged to someone unknown** in dreams, it means you are open to the world for new opportunities. You don't have any conditions but you want a new opportunity in waking life.
- If you **see engagement getting broke in dream**s, it could mean that you are broken in waking life and you need to forgive yourself as well as others in waking life.

- If you **see problems in getting engaged** in your dreams, it simply means you should and must address issues in your life so that you can live in peace.

First Kiss or First Sex

- If you dream about **having first kiss of your life** or kissing someone, this means you are happy and content in waking life.
- If you dream about **doing sex**, this means you want to get closer to someone in your waking life.

- If you dream about **others having kiss** in front of you, it symbolises love and affection in waking life.
- If you dream about **other having sex** in front you or you are watching someone else doing sex in your dreams, this means you are depending your life on someone's approval in waking life.
- If you dream **about kissing someone**, this means you are happy and content in waking life.

Getting or losing a job

- If you dream about **getting a new job**, it means some kind of change, growth or new opportunities in waking life.
- If you dream **about someone else getting a job**, this means you have some kind of insecurity or jealousy from someone in waking life.

- If you dream about **losing your job,** this means or shows anxiety in waking life or extra burdens that your job out on you in waking life.
- If you dream about **someone else losing their job**, this means you have unsettled grudge against someone in waking life.
- If you dream about **finding a job and not getting one,** it means your efforts are going down the drain in waking life.

Getting period or mensuration cycle

- If you dream about **getting your periods**, this means need for emotional release in waking life.
- If you see **the blood of your periods** in your dream, this means shedding of old habits or beliefs, or the beginning of a new chapter in life.
- If you see **not getting or delayed periods** in your dreams, this means fear of reproductive health in waking life.

I love You

- If someone **says I love you** in your dreams, it shows your desire for love and affection in waking life.
- If you **said I love you to someone** in your dream, it shows your desperation to get love and affection and attention in waking life.
- If **you are not able to say I love you** in your dream, it shows your disappointments in love in your waking life.

Marriage

- If you see yourself **getting married to someone known** in your dreams- it shows that you desire to be happy and have a loving partner in waking life.
- If you see yourself **getting married to someone unknown** or stranger in your dreams, it means you just came to know something about yourself that you didn't know before.
- If you see your **remarriage to someone known** in your dream, it means you are having anxiety issues and you are being restless in your waking life.
- If you see your **remarriage to someone unknown** in your dream, it means new beginnings will start in waking life.
- If you **see problems in getting married** in your dreams, it usually means the either you want to get married in waking life or you are anxious about your marriage in waking life.
- If you **see marriage getting broke** at the time of wedding in your dream, this usually means fear of change or commitment issues in waking life.

Migration

- If you see yourself **migrating to a different country in your dream**, this means that your subconscious is asking for a change in your life.
- If you see **yourself rejecting the migration** offer to a different country in your dream, this means your soul wants a change in your waking life but you are being stubborn and not realising the need for change in waking life.
- If you see **someone else migrating** to a different country in your dream, it means you want to giveaway some habits in waking life which will ultimately lead to peace.
- If you see **your closed people migrating** to a different country in your dream, this could mean unresolved conflicts in your relations in waking life.

Passing School or College or exams

- If you dream **about passing your school /Class/College** with good marks, it means accomplishments and achievements in waking life.
- If you dream **about failing the school/Class/College**, it means disappointments and discouragement in waking life.
- If you dream **about your convocation day**, it means achievement and success in waking life.

Promotion

- If you dream about **getting a promotion**, this means success and growth in career or relationship in waking life.

- If you dream about **not getting or losing a promotion**, it means you feel stuck either in career or relationship in waking life.
- If you dream about **someone else getting a promotion**, it represents anxiety or pressures from senior at work.
- If you dream about **someone else losing a promotion**, this means you are able to meet the target in your waking life.

Retirement

- If you **see getting retired** in your dream, it simply means unresolved conflicts at your work place and constant pressures at your workplace in waking life.
- If you **see others getting retired** in your dream, it also shows unresolved conflicts with people at your work place.

Voting

- If you see yourself **casting vote** in your dreams, this simply means you are concerned about your rights (could be about anything) in waking life.
- If you see **yourself denying to cast vote** in your dreams, this means you are expecting too much in your waking life.
- If you see **fighting an election** in dream, it means you are getting over ambitious and expect a lot of help from people around you in waking life.
- If you see **election items like EVM machines, election rally, ballot boxes etc**, this means there could be someone paperwork in waking life that you need to sort before it's too late.

Dreams about flowers

Floral dreams are usually happy dreams in general that shows happiness, prosperity and growth in waking life.
- If you **dream about the garden of flowers**, this shows some good news you will receive soon in waking life.
- If you dream **about bunch of flowers**, this shows you are internally happy or feel satisfied in waking life.
- If you dream about white flower, this might show some disappointments or influence or dominance of someone in waking life but in some situations, it shows peace is about to come.
- If you dream about **red flower**, this shows your idea of romance and romantic desires in waking life.
- If you dream about **yellow flowers**, this shows you are about to make new friends in waking life and also might be crushing on someone in waking life.
- If you dream about **orange flowers**, this shows you will be happy in the coming days in your waking life. Some fame you might receive in waking life.

- If you dream **about Black flowers**, this means be ready to receive some bad news about something in waking life or some major troubles.
- If you **don't see a flower in your dream** but see only the stems or mud, this shows you are looking to be happy in waking life but there is a delay in something but don't worry success is there at the end of the tunnel.

- If you see **someone is plucking the flower** in your dreams, it shows people are jealous of your capabilities or happiness in waking life.
- If you see **yourself planting a flowe**r in your dream, it's a good omen, this shows that you are laying foundation of something new in waking life which will prove to be positive for you in coming future. some new project or relationship.

If You see these specific flowers

Rose in dreams: this shows your passion and strength to do something in waking life. You have the courage. Move on.

Daisies in dreams: this is a symbol of good luck and good news in waking life. Also, you will be attracting peace in your situations.

Sunflower in dreams: this means you are attracting healing in your waking life.

Orchids in dreams: this shows celebration are coming in your waking life. Small or big, it doesn't matter but you will be celebrating something.

Lotus in dreams: this shows major financial abundance you are attracting in your life.

Green plants, grass, leaves and trees in dreams: this is the symbol of recovery from a prolonged illness or usually gives good health in waking life.

Travel dreams are usually connected to moments, moving forwards, transformations and new beginnings in waking life.

- If you dream about **making a travel plan**, this shows some kind of moment in your stagnant life in real.
- If you dream **about booking your tickets**, this means your soul is giving you permission to move forward.
- If you dream about **applying for a visa**, this shows your urge to make certain amendments in your waking life.
- If you dream about **packing your bags**, this shows readiness for change, transition, or a desire for a new beginning in your waking life.
- If you dream about **travelling with friends**, this shows your bond or

relationship with friends is taking a new shape in your waking life. Could be positive or negative.

- If you dream about **travelling with family**, this shows your bond or relationship with family is taking a new shape in your waking life. Could be positive or negative.
- If you dream about **travelling with strangers**, this shows you are trying to make new friends or relationship in waking life.

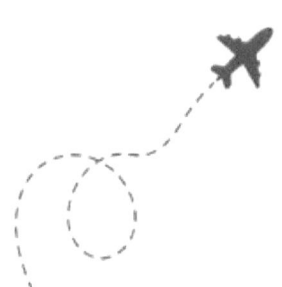

- If you dream about **travelling alone**, this shows the realisation that you are self-sufficient to face the challenges of the world or current loneliness in waking life.
- If you dream **about travelling to a historic place** or monument or ancient site, this shows or resembles the lost part of yourself or a forgotten responsibility in waking life. You need to focus, understand and fulfil that responsibility.
- If you dream about **going to your favourite place**, this is a good omen, you will get some good news in waking life soon.
- If you dream about **travelling to an unknown place**, this shows you are losing your purpose in life and you are not completely realising your worth.

- If you dream about **cancellation of travel plans** or not able to travel anywhere, this is a clear sign that you are suffering from inferiority complex and you need to come out of it in waking life.

- If you see yourself **travelling through auto or rikshaw,** this shows you fear for losing you wealth in waking life.
- If you see yourself **walking in your dream**, it shows that you are self-reliant in waking life, success is slow but you will definitely be going to get it.
- If you see **yourself going on a road trip**, this shows you will get a new opportunity and new direction in life which can give you quick success.
- If you see a **globe in your dream** and choosing the destination to travel, this shows you will soon get a travel opportunity.

I have already talked but seeing different places and different transportations in dreams earlier in the book.

Flying, Falling, running or attacking and more

These are very common dreams and almost everyone has seen this once in their life. These are the dreams of our feelings or reactions towards certain situations in our life.

Attacking dreams

The intensity of the attack in the dreams matters a lot. For some its normal but for some these dreams could come as a nightmare. Suddenly you see the dream and wakes up in the middle of the night. The intensity of the attack would show the intensity of your situation in waking life. If intensity is more, people take it as a nightmare as well as these are negative dreams or warning dreams.

You are being attacked by:

- If you dream about being **attacked by someone you love or your partner**, it means you are threatened by your own strong emotions for someone in your life.

- If you dream about being **attacked by someone stranger,** this shows your immunity system is weak and your body is fighting with something. Get a health check-up in waking life.
- If you dream about **being attacked by someone you know for a while**, it simply means you carry some kind of fear with in your heart and you really have to release that energy as it is now affecting your health in some or the other way.
- If you dream about **being attacked by an animal**, this is your instincts talking or warning you about something or someone in waking life. If you have doubts about something or someone, take that seriously now.

- If you dream about **being attacked by a pointed object,** this shows a strong enmity in waking life. Someone is not thinking good about you and can harm you in waking life. Just be careful of people's intentions.
- If you dream about **being attacked by a gun**, this shows you are experiencing some kind of confrontations in waking life.
- If you dream about being **attacked by fire**, this shows you are really angry on someone or something in real life and you really need to control that anger.

- If you dream about being **attacked inside your own house,** this questions your emotional or mental security in waking life. Maybe you feel insecure about somethings. You need to build your confidence.
- If you dream about **being attacked at some unknown place,** this shows that you are facing a lot of problems in waking life that you are not even aware about. A lot of problems might be coming towards you. Start analysing your situations and its outcomes.
- If you dream about **being attacked in some moving vehicle**, this shows life is moving towards some challenges or a health problem might become chronic.
- If you dream about **being attacked by God**, it simply means a spiritual attack is coming and you need to turn back to God for the relief.

You are attacking:

- If you dream **about attacking someone close**, this is a kind of negativity realising dream as you are going through stressful situations in waking life and it's a way of your mind to release out the negativity.
- If you dream **about attacking someone stranger**, this shows you are giving away the negativity in your

life and wants to be free from any disappointments you were facing for long.

- If you dream **about attacking someone with a pointed object**, this shows you are having some kind of hatred feeling towards someone and you soul or mind is trying to process that negativity.
- If you dream about **attacking someone with a Gun,** this simply means you have lost the trust on someone in waking life not necessarily the person you see attacking to.
- If you dream about **attacking an animal**, this shows for someone or something you killed your inner voice or conscious.
- If you dream **about attacking someone by fire**, this shows that your mind is releasing out all the anger it had for someone or something in waking life.
- If you dream about **attacking God in your dreams**, this shows you have broken all the rules and your arrogance is on the peak that you are not even scared from God or your past karma's actions.

Being found

- If you dream about **being found on the road**, this shows you are confident about the direction you chose for yourself in waking life.
- If you dream about being **found on the river side**, this shows you are confident about the emotional relationship that you are in, in your walking life.

- If you dream about **being found in dustbins**, this shows that you know where you want head towards in waking life but all your efforts are going wasted. Hold on, your time will come.
- If you dream about **people are searching for you** but not able to find you, this shows that you aren't sharing your thought and ideas about future with people. You are being a little secretive.

Being Late

- If you see **yourself getting late** for anything in your dreams, this means you are suffering from weight of expectations of other people in your waking life.
- If you see yourself **getting late because of someone else**, this means someone else is forcing or expecting you to do something which you really don't want to do in your waking life.
- If you see others **getting late in your dreams**, that means your inability to meet the expectations of others.
- If you are constantly looking or **staring at the watch** in your dream, this means you want to utilise your time in a better way in waking life

Being alone

If you see yourself being alone (sitting, standing or at some random place) this shows you are getting disappointed in waking life and there is someone sort of loneliness you are facing in your waking life.

Being Lost

- If you dream about **being lost at some strange place**, this usually shows anxiety or confused mind in waking life.
- If you dream about **being lost in your own house,** this shows you are anxious about your relationships in waking life.
- If you dream about b**eing lost with someone you know**, this means you are highly insecure about that person in waking life.
- If you dream **about being lost with someone stranger,** this means you are going insecure in general in your waking life. Could be about anything.

Burning

- If you see a **fire in your dream**, this shows that you are experiencing some major anger issues in your life.
- If you see you are **being burnt by fire** in your dream, this shows you did your own damage because of your anger and ego in your waking life.
- If you are **seeing a house or building on fire** in your dreams, this means you actions and ego has created a major destruction in your relationships.
- If you see **important papers are burning** in your dreams, this shows that your communications are going wrong in waking life.

Flying

- If you see **yourself flying in air** in your dreams, it shows freedom, liberation and control over your life. It also represents confidence in you and clear directions that where you want to head towards in waking life.
- If you see yourself **sitting on a cloud** in your dreams, it means you're seeking a quiet time to reflect on the happenings in your life.
- If you see yourself **flying on the broomstick** in your dreams, this shows that you are confident to sweep any negativity from your life and you will have a positive future ahead.
- If you see yourself **flying with someone** in your dreams, this shows you have an idea of where you want to take your life but you will require the help of someone and you are confident in your mind that person will help you. Whether the person will help you or not, it's a different story but you are confident.

Falling Dreams

- If you see yourself **falling from the mountain cliff** in your dreams, this shows a loss of control in some important situation in waking life.
- If you see yourself **falling from height into the water** in your dreams, this shows that you are unsure about your certain feelings about you career or emotional

life in your waking life. You feel overwhelmed with emotions.
- If you see **yourself falling on the road** in your dreams, this shows you feel insecure about something in waking life.
- If you see **someone pushed you from height** in your dreams, this shows you are highly anxious in your waking life.

Not able to move or stand still

- If you are **not able to move** in your dream, this shows feeling of isolations or loneliness in waking life.
- If you dream about that **you are forcing your body to move** but you are still not able to move, this shows that you are going through a lot of stress in waking life because of the people around you.
- If you dream about **that someone is holding you tight enough that you can't move**, this shows that someone has restricted your moments or growth in waking life and you are really stressed because of this.
- If you dream about that you have been **paralysed**, this is called sleep paralysis which can occur due to a lot of stress.

Running or Chasing

- If you dream about **running alone on the road**, this shows the desire to escape from the ongoing problems that you are facing in real life.

- If you dream about **running away from something,** this again shows you are trying to avoid a particular situation in your waking life.
- If you dream about **running behind a person**, this shows either you are longing for help in waking life or you are getting obsessed with someone in waking life not necessarily the one you were running behind in your dreams.
- If you dream about **running to catch a flight, bus or train,** this simply shows you want to hide yourself and wants a complete change in your situations in real life. You are tired and can't handle it any further.
- If you dream about **running towards food**, this shows you are wasting your basic necessities in waking life and you need to have more understanding of what is required in waking life rather than what you want.
- If you feel **someone is chasing you in your dreams**, this shows that you are suffering from depression and high anxiety in waking life and you could be on the medication for that.
- If you feel **an animal is changing you in your dreams**, this shows that your gut or inner voice is trying to tell you or warn you about something but you are avoiding it because of your desire, desperation or lack of understanding.

Accident

- If you see your **own accident in dream**, this shows feeling of regret or guilt in waking life.
- If you see **Somone else's accident in dream**, this is a very inauspicious dream as per expert. One needs to avoid any new work or signing a new contract in waking life.

Asthma or choking

If you see yourself suffering from asthma or choking in your dreams, this shows you are feeling suffocated in some situation in waking life.

Blood pressure (BP)issues or heart problem

- If you see yourself **suffering from BP issues** in your dream, this reflects your emotional stress in waking life.
- If you see **others suffering from BP issues** in your dreams, this show that others are troubling you or giving you stress in waking life.

- If you see yourself **having a heart attack** in your dream, this shows lack of support or lack of acceptance in waking life.
- If you see others **or someone else getting a heart attack** in your dream, this shows lack of support in waking life.

Cuts and scratches

- If you see a **cut or scratch on your body** in your dreams, this shows you have such negative thoughts that you hide from others.
- If you see a **cut or scratch on someone else's body** in your dream, this shows something painful is being repressed in waking life. Or someone else is having negative thoughts about you.

Cough/Cold

- If you see **yourself having cough or cold** in your dream, this shows that you are carrying something with you which you need to get rid of from your life.
- If you see others **having cough or cold** in your dreams, this show that you think about others that they are having unnecessary pain and they need to cut down negativity from their life.

Cancer or other chronic disease

- If you see yourself **suffering from cancer** or any other chronic disease in your dream, this shows a

stressful situation in waking life that you need to manage.
- If you see your **closed one suffering from cancer** or any other chronic disease in your dream, this shows you need to manage things for others who are suffering from some stressful situation in waking life
- If you see a **stranger suffering from cancer** or any other chronic disease in your dream, this shows an unexpected stressful situation is coming your way.

Diarrhoea/ lose motions

- If you see **yourself suffering from diarrhoea** in your dream, this means powerful release of old emotions in waking life
- If you **see others suffering from diarrhoea** in your dream, this means others are reminding you of your strong past memories in waking life

Diabetes

If you dream about getting diabetes, this shows sacrifice you make or willing to make in waking life.

Fever

- If you dream about **having high fever in your dreams**, this simply means you are low on your energy or craving affection in waking life.
- If you dream about **others having high fever in your dreams,** this means others might need your attention in waking life.

Getting pimples

- If you see **yourself getting or having pimples** in dreams, this shows some embarrassing situations or social embarrassment in waking life.
- If you see **others getting pimples** in your dreams, this shows your fear of facing people in waking life.

Headaches

- If you dream about **having a severe headache** in dream, this could actually be hypnic headache, a type of headache that happens during sleep only. Can usually happen between 1am to 3 am and can wake up people. If you don't experience this then it simply means stress in waking life.
- If you dream about **others having headaches** in dreams, this means others require your help in their stressful situations.

Hospitalization (but not ICU)

- If you see **yourself hospitalised in your dream**, it means challenges are part of your daily routine or you need to take care of your health before it becomes big in waking life.
- If you see a **closed one hospitalised in your dream**, it means you need to take care of their health in waking life.

Injections

- If you see **yourself getting an injection** in your dreams, this shows the difficulty you are facing in allowing something in your life or accepting something in your waking life.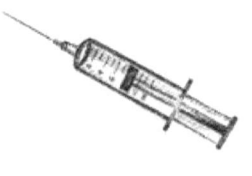
- If you see **others getting an injection** in your dreams, this means you want to stop someone from taking certain action in their life.

Kidney issues

If you see a kidney related issue in your dreams, this shows monetary gains in waking life esp. if you have seen kidney stones.

Losing teeth

- If you dream about **losing one or two teeth**, this shows child birth or a spiritual rebirth.
- If you dream about **losing all your teeth**, this shows that you have recently lost something very dear to you, could be you job or a loved one.
- If you dream about **extracting your own teeth**, this symbolises that you need to cut down ties with someone who is adding too much of negativity in your waking life.

- If you see yourself **brushing your teeth**, this shows that you are gaining power and being assertive in your actions in waking life.

Losing hair or hair fall

- If you see **yourself bald** in your dreams, this shows actual hair loss in waking life or losing your beauty in waking life.

- If you see yourself **having hair fall** in your dreams, this usually means loss of sexual appeal in waking life.
- If you see **someone else losing their hair** in your dreams, this shows your lack of interest in someone in waking life.

Losing blood

Blood in dreams symbolises sadness, struggle or loss.

- If you see **yourself losing blood in** dreams, this indicates a struggle that you are dealing with in your waking life.
- If you see **others losing blood** in dreams, this shows that you are processing a loss of someone in waking life.

Medications

- If you see **yourself taking pills** or medicines in dreams, this shows you are attracting some healing in your life.
- If you see **others taking pills or medicines** in dreams, this shows others will extend some support in your life.

Mouth infections

- If you dream about **suffering from mouth infections**, this shows a disaster or business or job loss in waking life.
- If you dream about **others suffering from mouth infections**, this shows the loss could be because of others in waking life.

Pain in the body parts

- If you dream about **having pain in body parts**, pain is associated with very strong emotions such as hate and anger and if you see having pain in any of your body part in your dreams then it means you are having such strong emotions for someone or something in waking life.
- If you dream **about others having pain in body parts**, that you have the feeling of anger or frustrations towards that specific person.

Small Pox

- Dreaming of small pox symbolises unexpected gain, old money could be recovered. It doesn't matter whether you are having a small pox in your dreams or someone else getting that.

Stomach infections or indigestion

Dreaming about stomach infections represents a new lifestyle or change in current lifestyle in waking life.

Surgery/operations

- If you see **yourself doing an operation** in your dream, this shows you are trying hard to take your power back in your hands in waking life.
- If you see **getting operated** in your dream, this shows your powerlessness in waking life.
- If you see others **getting operated in your dream**, this shows that you are not satisfied with the ways you are living your life and there is a need for change.

Vomiting

- If you dream about **vomiting lying on the floor**, this shows you need to realise and have better understanding of the negativity in your life.
- If you see **yourself doing vomiting in your dream**, this shows that you need to release the negativity from your life even if you need to withdraw yourself from certain situation or you need to cut ties with certain people.

- If you see **others vomiting in dreams**, this shows someone is trying to evoke feeling to disgust or uncomfortableness in your life.
- If you see **wiping the vomiting in dream**, this shows the embarrassment you are facing because of others in your life.

Ventilator/ICU

- If you see **yourself on ventilator or ICU** in your dreams, this shows you are going through some traumatic stress in waking life.
- If you see a **closed one on ventilator or ICU** in your dreams, take it as a warning and take care of person's health in waking life.
- If you see a **stranger on ventilator or ICU** in your Dream, this means an unexpected big problem is coming towards you.

Examinations

Examination dreams are very common dreams that the person sees. Mostly failing in an exam or having a distinction. Exams are connected to your life obstacles in waking life. The challenges you face or fears that you have.

- If you see **yourself failing in an exam** in your dream, this shows that you are facing a stressful situation in waking life and that is bothering you a lot.

- If you see **others failing in an exam** in your dream, this shows your fears related to life.
- If you see **preparing for an exam** in your dream, this shows fears for not being prepared for an upcoming challenge in your waking life.
- If you see **writing an exam** in your dream, this means you will soon face a test in your life where you need to take an important decision.

- If you see **yourself passing an exam** in your dream, this shows you have done well in dealing with the problems in waking life.
- If you see **others passing an exam** in your dream, this shows your mind and subconscious actively working for your success.

Beauty services in dreams resembles relaxing and pampering in your dreams. This also symbolises your social communications or circle in your dreams. Sometimes it also focussed on self-esteem issues and independence.

Facials

- If you see **yourself getting a facial done** in your dreams, this shows you have major self-esteem issues and fighting with yourself in waking life
- If you see yourself **others getting a facial** in your dreams, this means your self-esteem got hurt because of others in waking life.
- If you see **preparing yourself for getting a facial** in your dream, this shows that you don't want to embarrass yourself in front of others in waking life so you are working on yourself in waking life.
- If you see yourself **putting a facemask or scrubbing** yourself in dreams, this shows you are

pampering yourself in waking life or there is a need that you must pamper yourself in waking life.

Waxing/shavings

- If you see yourself **getting a waxing/ shaving** done in your dreams, this shows you are making a minor life changing decision.
- If you see **others getting a waxing /shaving done** in your dreams, this shows loss of your independence
- If you see **waxing or shaving material** in your dreams, this shows you need to monitor your decisions.

Manicure

- If you see yourself **getting a manicure done** in your dreams, this shows the person is having a feeling of high self-esteem and trust the people around them.
- If you see **others getting a manicure** done in your dreams, this shows there is low self-esteem and lack of trust in a person in waking life.
- If you see **yourself getting your nails done** (nail pain or nail art) in your dreams, this shows you are busy in serving others but you should focus on yourself in waking life.

Pedicure.

- If you see yourself **getting a pedicure done** in your dreams, its simply the sign of relaxation and self-care in waking life.
- If you see **others getting a pedicure done** in your dreams, this shows some kind of transformation is coming.

Tattoo

- If you see **yourself getting your first tattoo** done in your dreams, this shows you are trying to define yourself among people in waking life.
- If you see **yourself getting multiple tattoos done** in your dreams, this simply shows your control over your body, attitude and actions. You do what you feel like doing in waking life.
- If you see yourself **removing a tattoo** from your body in your dreams, this shows you are going to find yourself in some situation because of your own actions in real life.
- If you see **others getting a tattoo** done in your dreams, this shows that other people want to communicate certain things to you in waking life.

- If you see **others removing their tattoo** in your dreams, this shows your social circle might be maintaining distance from you because of some of your personality traits.

Eyebrows or removing facial hair

- If you see yourself **getting an eyebrow done** in your dreams, this shows you are improving your social communication in waking life.
- If you see **others getting an eyebrow done** in your dreams, this shows your social circle is trying to improve their connections with you in your waking life.
- If you see **thick eyebrows** in your dreams, this shows success and also social communication in waking life.

Piercing

- If you see y**ourself getting a piercing done** in your dreams, this shows a desire for a change or transformation.
- If you see **others getting a piercing done** in your dreams, this shows pain or blockages given my others in your growth.

Hair services

- If you see yourself **getting a haircut done**, this shows that you are taking control of your life in your own hands.

- If you see yourself **getting a hair treatment / extension** done, this shows you are trying to modify the situation or opportunities in waking life.

- If you see yourself getting a **hair extension/ treatment done**, this shows you are looking and accepting the opportunities that you are getting in your life.

Beauty treatments For Face and Body

- If you see **yourself going to a dermatologist** for a consultation in your dreams, this resembles healing and taking time for yourself to pamper yourself in walking life.
- If you see yourself **going for a laser therapy** in your dream, this symbolises clarity and truth in waking life.
- If you see **yourself getting a laser therapy** in your dream, this shows you already know the truth and now you need to decide the direction to take forward. Mostly its connected with your social circle.
- If you **see yourself buying a lot of medicines** for your skin in your dreams, this shows you will be relaxed in the coming future as you are attracting healing in waking life.
- If you see **yourself buying a lot of skin care** in your dream, this shows you want to be socially accepted in your circle and also you are working hard for it.

- If you see **yourself taking needles** on your face in your dreams, this shows you are not comfortable with how people treat you in waking life.

For teeth

- If you see yourself **getting a tooth extracted by a dentist** in your dreams, this shows you are able to correct some kind of communication that had gone wrong in the past in waking life.
- If you see yourself **getting a bristle** in your dreams, this is a positive dream which shows that you are trying to protect
- yourself and the way you communicate with people around you. You think before you speak in waking life.

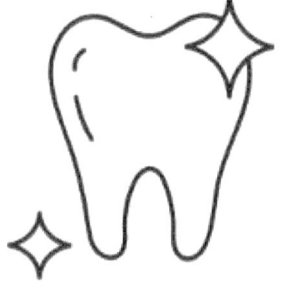

- If you see **yourself removing a bristle** in your dream, this shows you are speaking before you actually think what you are saying. Your words could hurt others around you.
- If you see yourself **going to a dentist** in your dream, this could mean that you are going anxious about your communication in waking life and you have the intention to improve it.

For your weight

- If you see **yourself getting a bariatric surgery** or weight loss surgery in your dreams, this shows you are craving respect and appreciation from people around you. And you want it any how in waking life.
- If you see **yourself visiting a doctor for consultation** to reduce your weight in your dream, this show that you are concerned about your image in your social circle and thinking ways to improve that.
- If you see **yourself taking weight reduction pills** or medicines in your dreams, this shows either you really want to reduce weight or its your desire to control a particular situation that might affect your image in waking life.
- If you see **yourself taking weight reduction injections** in your dreams, this shows either you really want to reduce weight desperately or its your desire to control a particular situation that might affect your image in waking life.

Eyes

- If you dream about **buying new specs or glasses** for yourself, this shows you are seeing things clearly in waking life.
- If you dream about **going to an Ophthalmologist** for eye surgery to remove your glasses or eye number, this shows you should change the way you see a particular situation in waking life. You need to analyse all its facts clearly.
- If you see yourself **putting an eye, drop in your eyes** in your dream, this means you need emotional healing in waking life.
- If you see **putting an eye, drop in someone else eye** in your dreams, this means you think your emotional healing is dependent on others.

Buying

- If you see yourself **buying any fruits or vegetables** in your dreams, this shows a transfer or moving to a new place suddenly.
- If you see buying **yourself an electronic item** in your dreams, this shows your need to communicate with people.
- If you see yourself **buying new clothes** in your dreams, this means you want to change people's perception that how they look at you in waking life.
- If you see yourself **buying makeup** in your dreams, this means you are trying to hide some of your secret from people around you in waking life.
- If you see yourself **buying home decor** in your dreams, this means you will soon be investing in a property in your waking life.

- If you see yourself **buying any sweets** in your dreams, this means you will soon be receiving any good news in waking life.
- If you see **yourself buying any groceries** in your dreams, this means you are focussing on basic necessities of life.
- If you see yourself **buying a property or land** in your dreams this means you will gain some financial abundance in waking life.

Cooking

- If you see yourself **chopping the vegetables** in your dream, this shows your desire to grow in waking life and to get any possible opportunity for your growth.
- If you see **yourself cooking in your dream**, this shows your creativity and ability to create a new opportunity or innovate your existing opportunities.

- If you see **yourself baking in your dream**, this shows the feeling of being sensual in waking life.

Celebrating Birthdays

- If you see **yourself celebrating your own birthday** in your dream, this shows a huge loss or bad times coming ahead in life.

- If you see **others celebrating their birthday** in your dreams, this shows you need to be careful as someone close can give you bad news in life.

- If you see a **stranger celebrating their birthday** in your dreams, this shows an unexpected loss will come in your life.
- If you see a **celebrity celebrating their birthday** in your dreams, this shows your biggest fear is taking shape and soon you will face its consequences in waking life.

Dancing

- If you see yourself **dancing alone in your dream**, this shows you are happy and cheerful in life but afraid to share that with people.

- If you see yourself **dancing in front of people** in your dream, this shows you are happy and cheerful as a personality in waking life.
- If you see yourself **dancing with people** in your dream, this shows you happiness depends on your relationship and love to move along with people

Drinking

- If you see **yourself drinking water** in your dream, this could signify your need for refreshment or rejuvenation in waking life.
- If you see yourself **drinking juice** in your dream, this shows good health and good vitality of life.

- If you see **yourself drinking alcohol** in your dream, this shows you are going to achieve something big in your coming future in waking life.
- If you see yourself **drinking any other drinks** in your dream, this shows your desire to be more socially active in your waking life.

Driving

- If you see yourself **driving in your dreams**, this means you are in control over the directions you are heading towards in waking life.
- If you see yourself **flying a plane** in your dreams, this shows your desire for freedom in waking life.
- If you see yourself **sailing a boat** or ship in your dreams, this means you need to gain balance in waking life.

- If you see yourself **doing an accident or crash** in your dreams this means a feeling of regret or guilt in waking life.

Eating

- If you see yourself **eating home food** in your dream, this shows your nurturing and caring nature in waking life.
- If you see yourself **eating outside food** in your dream, this shows that you want something in your waking life that others have.
- If you see yourself **eating flesh** in your dream, this shows your desire will bring disasters in your life. Be careful of what you wish for. And some health issues are about to come.
- If you see yourself **eating cake/ ice-cream/ sweets** in your dream, this is a pure symbol of love for others in your waking life.

Earning

- If you see a **bag full of money in your dreams**, this shows that give importance to your self-worth in your waking life.

- If you see **earning a lot of money** in your dreams, this shows you have confidence in your capabilities and you are hopeful that the situation will turn in your favour.

- If you see **others earning a lot of money** in your dreams, this means you are scared that situation might not turn in your favour.
- If you see others **returning your money** in your dreams, this shows that you will get the reward of your efforts soon in waking life.

Feelings

- If you are **feeling happy in your dream**, this shows your happy state of mind in waking life or soon you will be attracting happiness.
- If you are **feeling loved in your dreams**, this shows that you are content and happy with your relationships in waking life.
- If you are **feeling jealous in** your dream, this shows you are actually feeling jealous of someone in waking life.
- If you are **feeling sad or heart broken** in dream, this shows that you are actually sad and facing disappointments in waking life.

Hiding

- If you see **yourself hiding yourself from person or situation in** dreams, this shows the embarrassing situations you are facing or about to face in waking life.
- If you see **yourself hiding some conversation from people** in dreams, this shows you are not completely showing your heart out. A part of your personality is hidden from people in your waking life

- If you see yourself **hiding anything else from people** in your dreams, this shows you never shares 100% of the things in your heart or in your mind.

Hugging

- If you see **yourself hugging someone** close in your dream, this shows the need for an emotional support in waking life.
- If you see yourself **hugging someone stranger** in your dreams, this shows the need to forgive or be forgiven in waking life.

Investing

- If you see investing your money anywhere in **bank, funds, stocks etc in your dreams**, this means you have the desire to increase your wealth in waking life.

- If you see that you have invested your money somewhere and **had a huge loss** in your dreams, this shows your insecurity related to your financial position in waking life.

Laughing/Crying

- If you see **yourself smiling in the dream**, this shows happiness and contentment in waking life.

- If you see **yourself laughing in the dream**, this shows one important desire got fulfilled in waking life.
- If you **see yourself crying in the dream**, this shows suppressed emotions in waking life.

Running/Jogging

- If you see **yourself running on the road** in your dreams, this shows you are ready to take on new challenges that is coming in the fulfilment of your desire.
- If you see **yourself running on water** in your dream, this shows your urge to climb a ladder of achievements in your waking life.
- If you see yourself **running on cloud** in your dream, this shows you are quickly to fall in love and quickly move out of love.
- If you see yourself **running inside your house** in your dream, this shows you are not able to process the reality as it is in waking life.

- If you see **yourself running to reduce weight** in your dream, this shows you have doubts that the project you are working on will materialize in future or no.
- If you see **yourself going for a morning jog** in your dream, this shows speedy recovery in your health or other areas in waking life.
- If you see **yourself running on a treadmill** in your dream, this is a sign of frustration in waking life. You are just not happy about something that is going on in your waking life.

Sitting

- If you see yourself **sitting on a couch or chair** in your dream, this shows relaxation and comfort in waking life.
- If you see yourself **sitting on bed** in your dream, this shows you are at peace in your waking life.
- If you see yourself **sitting under the tree** in your dream, this shows a feeling of security from an unsettled position in your waking life.
- If you see yourself **sitting near any water body** in your dream, it shows that you are processing some kind of emotional trouble or situation in waking life.

- If you see yourself **sitting under the water** in your dream, this shows the emotional troubles have taken over your mental peace in your life.
- If you see yourself **sitting under the sun** in your dreams, this is a very good omen, this shows you are happy and content in your waking life and all your desires would be met.
- If you see yourself **sitting on the road** in your dreams, this shows that you are evaluating the purpose of your life or next step ahead to take in waking life.

Sleeping

- If you see **yourself sleeping on a couch** or chair in your dream, this shows the feeling of comfort, ease and relaxations in waking life.
- If you see **yourself sleeping on a bed** in your dream, this shows comfort, feeling of security and personal boundaries you have created in waking life.
- If you see **yourself sleeping under the tree** in your dream, this shows desires for taking a break from your daily life.
- If you see **yourself sleeping under the sun** in your dream, this shows the feeling of hope and renewal in the waking life. Like everything will be fine and shows the person's positivity in waking life.
- If you see **yourself sleeping on the road** in your dreams, this could mean that you are able to anticipate future scenarios and thinking to walk on that or no.

Watching

- If you see **yourself watching a movie/play** or any other show in your dream, it means a truth is about to be revealed in waking life.
- If you see **yourself watching a crime** in your dream, this shows a warning that you will encounter a news that wont in your favour in waking life. Bitter truths of life.
- If you see yourself **watching something weird** in your dream, this means something will come in front of you that you already knew but pretending to ignore it for a while.

Studying/Reading

- If you see **yourself studying in** your dreams, this shows your desires for knowledge and self-improvement in waking life.

- If you see **yourself reading a book** in your dreams, this represents knowledge wisdom and insights about life in your real life.
- If you see **yourself reading a magazine** in your dreams, this shows your involvement in gossips in waking life.

- If you see yourself **reading a newspaper** in your dream, this shows you want to have knowledge about worldly events and you are curious to know everything.
- If you see yourself **reading a thesis** in your dream, this shows your desire to study further in waking life esp. with a change of location.
- If you see yourself **reading a message** in your dream, this shows you are expecting a news in waking life. Something that is important to you.
- If you see yourself **reading an email** in our dream, this shows you might be getting a new and a big opportunity in your life.

Singing

- If you see **yourself singing in bathroom** in your dream, this shows that you are trying to hide some happiness and feeling about how you feel from people in waking life.
- If you see yourself **singing in front of people** in your dream, this shows you are ready to share the happy news and your personal feelings with everyone.

Stealing

- If you see **yourself stealing any valuable thing** in your dreams, this shows feeling robbed or cheated in real life in some way in waking life.
- If you see yourself **stealing any basic necessities** in your dreams, this shows you are struggling to survive in waking life but problem is because of others.
- If you see **yourself stealing something from a closed one** thing in your dreams, this is a feeling that someone has cheated you emotionally.
- If you see yourself **stealing something from a stranger** in your dreams, this means don't trust people that easily in waking life.

Toilet

- If you see **yourself using a restroom** in your dream, this means you are ready to move on from any negative emotions in waking life.
- If you see **yourself passing a stool (poop)** in your dream, this shows your life needs a big transformation and you need to do hard work towards it.
- If you see yourself **passing urine** in your dream, this shows you need to let something go.
- If you see yourself **stepping over a poop or urine** in your dream, this shows that universe is giving you the hint to look or analyse your life as it need some changes.

Thinking

If you see yourself **thinking deep** about someone thing in your dream, this dream shows the meaning of the thoughts that might be bothering you in waking life.

Talking

- If you see yourself **talking to strangers** in your dreams, this shows unknown or unfamiliar aspect of yourself.
- If you see **yourself talking to closed ones** in your dreams, this shows you are trying to improve your personal relationships in waking life.

- If you see **yourself talking to a therapist** in your dreams, this shows you are going through some emotional issues and you need help in waking life.
- If you see **yourself talking to your boss** in your dreams, this shows you are expecting a promotion in waking life.
- If you see yourself **talking to colleagues** or subordinates in your dreams, this shows you are doing well at the given task in office in waking life.
- If you see **yourself talking to God in your dreams,** this shows your silent prayers in waking life.

- If you see yourself **talking to a devil** in your dreams, this shows you are yourself inviting some big problem in your life.
- If you see yourself **talking to dead people** in your dreams, this shows you are internally fighting with yourself to prove you right in front of everyone in waking life but actually it's an ego game.

Walking

- If you see **yourself walking on the road** in your dreams, this shows you know your future path and you are working towards it in waking life.
- If you see **yourself walking on water** in your dream, this resembles high level of self-confidence and ability to overcome challenges in waking life.
- If you see **yourself walking on cloud** in your dream, this is a good dream as it shows that you are deeply in love with someone in real life.
- If you see yourself **walking inside your house** in your dream, this could mean that you want to explore your mind in more depth in waking life.
- If you see yourself **walking to reduce weight** in your dream, this shows that you are facing a stressful situation in waking life.
- If you see **yourself going for a morning walk** in your dream, this shows progress especially in the area of health in waking life.

- If you see yourself **walking on a treadmill** in your dream, this shows you want something in your waking life and you are desperately moving towards it.

- If you dream **about walking alone**, this shows feeling of empowerment or independence in waking life.
- If you dream **about walking with someone**, this shows your heart is going towards someone in waking life.
- If you dream **about walking holding hand of someone**, this shows how deeply you feel about someone in waking life not necessarily the one you saw in your dreams.
- If you dream about **being injured and still walking**, this means you are hurt or soon be hurt by some actions of others. Don't expect much.
- If you dream about **walking in rain**, this shows or symbolises your inner peace.
- If you dream about **walking in snow**, this shows the challenges, you are going to encounter in your waking life.

- If you dream about **walking in dirty water**, this shows you are burdened with negative emotions and you need to release that.
- If you dream about **walking in mud or desert,** this shows that there is some situation in waking life that you are stuck in.
- If you dream about **walking in dark**, this shows that you are suffering from depression, or facing some kind of mystery in waking life that you aren't able to solve.
- If you dream about **walking in the mountains**, this shows the progress towards your goal.

Writing

- If you see **yourself writing a diary** or journal in your dreams, this shows that you want to explore your own mind and gain insights of your own thoughts.
- If you see **yourself writing a book** in your dreams, this shows creativity and desire to share your knowledge with people in waking life.
- If you see **yourself writing a magazine** in your dreams, this could mean you are about to enter a new relationship in waking life.
- If you see **yourself writing a newspaper** in your dream, this shows you a big news in your waking life that you are hiding from people.

- If you see **yourself writing a thesis** in your dream, this shows your desire for knowledge and enrolment into a new course in your waking life.
- If you see yourself **writing a message** in your dream, this shows that you want to convey your feelings to someone in waking life.
- If you see yourself **writing an email** in your dream, this shows you want to apply for some new opportunity in waking life.

Sunrise

- If you see yourself watching a sunrise in your dreams, this shows new beginnings, hope and positivity in waking life.
- If you see others watching a sunrise in your dreams, that you wish and pray happiness and new beginnings for others in waking life.
- If you are watching a sunrise with your closed people, this means the new beginnings are coming for the entire family. You will attract some kind of celebrations at home.
- If you are watching the sunrise with strangers, this shows you will meet new people in your life that will prove to be positive influence in your waking life.

Sun

If you see the sun in your dream (not rise or set), it means you will receive positivity, good news and healing in waking life.

Sunsets

- If you see **yourself watching a sunset** in your dreams, this could mean end of something may be a job or relationship or anything else but something will end in waking life.
- If you see **others watching a sunset** in your dreams, that something bad is about to happen to a person you are close to.
- If you are **watching a sunset with your closed people**, this could mean your family has to suffer in your waking life.

- If you are **watching the sunset with strangers**, this means a person will hamper your progress in your waking life, not necessarily the same person you saw in your dreams.

Moonrise

- If you see **yourself watching a moonrise** in your dreams, this shows a divine blessing or a happy marriage or soon be attracting a good partner in your waking life.

- If you see **others watching a moonrise** in your dreams, this means someone who is closed to you have received a divine blessing.

- If you are **watching a moonrise with your closed people**, this means your family will receive blessings from the universe.
- If you are watching **the moonrise with strangers**, this shows you are attracting a soulmate in your waking life.

Moon

If you see only moon in your dreams (not rise or sets), it means you will attract an emotional healing very soon in waking life

Moonset

- If you see **yourself watching a moonset** in your dreams, this is a symbol of change in your life. Whether good or bad but a change will come.
- If you see **others watching a moonset** in your dreams, this means the change that will come is because of others in your life.

- If you are **watching a moonset with your closed people,** this shows that the change will come is because of your family in your waking life.

- If you are **watching the moonset with strangers**, this shows the change that will come is because of someone that you don't even know completely in waking life.

New moon

If you see a new moon night in your dreams, this shows or represents new beginnings in waking life.

Stars

- If you **see stars in your dreams**, it's a positive omen, you will receive good news and success in waking life.
- If you **see a broken star** in your dream, this means your growth will time in waking life.
- If you dream **about watching stars from telescope,** this means you are expecting a growth in your life and you see it coming in your waking life.

Rainbow

If you see a rainbow in your dream, this is a good omen and bring in good fortune in waking life. This is a very positive dream and can bring in growth and success in your life.

Galaxy

If you see **a galaxy in your** dreams, it shows you are about to make new friends and contacts in your waking life.

Heatwave/ Cold wave

If you see or feel a heatwave or cold wave in your dreams, it means some uncomfortable situation you are facing or will face in waking life. May be someone is betraying you and you need to be careful.

Indoor games

- If you see **yourself playing any board game** in your dreams, this signifies your progress in waking life.
- If you see **yourself playing any cards** in your dreams, this shows you are getting inclined towards gambling in real life.
- If you see **yourself playing any hide and seek** in your dreams, this shows you are being playful and mischief in waking life.

- If you see yourself **solving a puzzle** in your dream, this shows you are trying to solve a mystery in waking life.
- If you see yourself **playing any other game** in your dreams, this means you are keeping secrets in your life.

- If you see yourself **playing a video game on PSV or Mobile** in your dreams, this shows that you desire to escape from your current situation or you want to take the control of your choice.
- If you see yourself **playing with a toy** in your dreams, this shows your playful side in waking life. You are taking things in a light manner and want to enjoy in real life.

Outdoor dreams

- If you see **yourself playing any cricket** in your dreams, this means you have the courage to achieve success in waking life.
- If you see yourself **playing any badminton/tennis** in your dreams, this shows you need to relax more in your waking life.
- If you see yourself **playing with ball** in your dreams, this shows you require balance in your life before moving ahead in any situation.

- If you see yourself **playing any other outdoor game** in your dreams, this suggests sadness within you in your waking life.

- If you see yourself **skating in your dreams**, this shows that you are in danger and about to lose some important opportunity in waking life.

Game or Toy shop

- If you see a **toy store in your dreams**, this shows you want things to be simple in your waking life and you want to feel lighter and don't want to take unnecessary stress in waking life.
- If you see **buying a toy from a toy store** in your dreams, this shows you have found a solution for your problems and things will be fine in the coming time.

Horror dreams

Horror dreams are the symbol of on-going stress, trauma, negativity, supressed emotions or heavy food.

Ghost/evil spirits

- If you **see a ghost in your dreams**, this shows the situations in your life is gone out of hands and now it's affecting your soul.
- If you see **talking to a ghost in your dream**, this shows there is something about the situation in waking life that is haunting you and you are analysing it.
- If you see a **ghost is attacking you in your dreams,** this is a bad omen shows a chronic health problem or death.

- If you see **two or more ghosts in your dreams**, this shows the negative situation that you are facing is

giving you depressions or trauma of some kind in waking life.
- If you see **a ghost coming out of his grave**, this means the problem that you are facing in waking life is not going to end soon, something more will come soon that can give you more anxiety.

Horror experiences in your dream,

- If you feel that **someone is sleeping next to you** in your dreams, this shows you are facing major depression in waking life and requires help.
- If you feel that **someone invisible is chasing you** in your dreams, this means you are running away from your own feelings and trying to avoid it but soon you will be facing it.
- If you feel **someone invisible is pushing you** in your dreams, this means you are suffering mentally because of your life situation and blaming it on others in waking life.

Blood

- If you see **blood stains on your clothes** in your dreams, this shows some kind of injury and pain in your waking life.

- If you see **blood in your house** in your dreams, this shows that there will be a loss in your family (could be of money or person)
- If you see **blood on any of your body part** in your dreams, this means you will encounter some major health trouble in waking life.
- If you see **blood anywhere else in your dreams**, this shows the pain that is about to come in waking life.

Flesh

- If you see **flesh of an animal** in your dream, this shows your aggression and uncivilised way of dealing with a person or situation in waking life.
- If you see **flesh of a human** in your dream, to the contrary to the above dream, this shows materialistic progress and gain in your waking life.

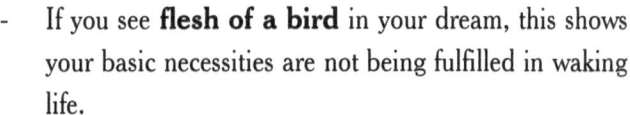

- If you see **flesh of a bird** in your dream, this shows your basic necessities are not being fulfilled in waking life.
- If you see **yourself eating flesh** in your dream, this shows major health trouble waits for you in waking life. Also, your desire will bring disasters in your life

Suicide

- If you see **yourself committing suicide** in your dreams, this shows you are suffering from higher stress and dealing with suicidal thoughts in waking life.
- If you see **others committing suicide** in your dreams, this shows you are suffering from emotionally difficult situation in life.

Spooky places/Haunted houses

- If you see a **spooky place or a haunted house from outside** in your dreams, this represents the negativity of the people that you dealt with in the past. You are not able to get over that.
- If you see a **spooky place or a haunted house from inside in your dreams**, this represents the negativity of the people you are dealing with in day-to-day life. You need to be extra careful in dealing with them.

Spooky stuff

- If you see **a bat or group of bats** resting on a tree in your dreams, this shows you need to trust your guts and follow your instincts in waking life.
- If you see **a bat or group of bats flying** in your dreams, this shows you need to trust your guts and follow your instincts in waking life as you are surrounded by negative people and situations.

- If you see a **dead tree without any leaves** and with dead branches in your dreams, this shows that something in your life is coming to its end. This could be a relation, a job or anything else.

- If you see a **hand with extremely long nails** in your dreams, this shows that you aren't able to let go something in waking life.
- If you see a **dark night with clouds coming over moon or stars** in your dreams, this shows problems that you aren't able to see clearly in waking life.
- If you see a **spider web** in your dreams, this represents emotions that you feel stuck at in your current situation.
- If you see a **spider in your dream**, this is a warning that you should not trust someone in waking life. You need to be careful.
- If you see **a lighting in your dream**, this shows some kind of unexpected health issues in waking life

Skeleton

- If you see a **complete skeleton** in your dreams, this shows some chronic health issues that you will be facing in your waking life.

- If you see **parts of skeleton** in your dreams, this shows the health problem mainly in the part of the body which you see as the skeleton part in your dream. Like if you see a bone of a skeleton that shows you will have health trouble related to bones in waking life.

Dreaming about Ex or lover or crush

Dreaming about an ex

- If you are **thinking about your ex in waking life** and see the person(ex) in your dreams, this means nothing as you are overthinking and that what is coming in your dreams.

- If you haven't **thought about your ex for at least two months** and see him in your dreams, this means you mind is moving towards the closure and it started processing the old memories. Soon it will fade away.

- If you **haven't thought about your ex at all** and see him in your dreams, this is a telepathy message and soon you could hear it from the person or they might have thought about you recently.

- If you **have recently broken the relationship** and see your ex in dreams, this means that your mind is trying to process the pain.

Dreaming about current lover

If you are dating or in relationship with someone and dream about the person, this means it's the feeling of admiration and growing feelings with the person.

Crush

If you like a person and you want to get into a relationship with that person in waking life and see the person in dreams, this shows your inner desires with the person.

Infidelity

- If you dream about **cheating your partner (many times)** in your dream, this shows you are ignoring your relationship or ignored your relationship in your past.
- If you dream about **your partner is cheating on you (many times)** in your dream, this shows your insecurities related to your relationship in waking life

Camera

- If you see **yourself clicking a picture** in your dream, this shows you are trying to create or recall a past incident in waking life.
- If you see **others clicking your picture** in your dreams, this shows the impact of your past memories in your current life.
- If you see a **cracked camera** in your dream, this shows you badly want to forget some past incidences but not able to.
- If you see **someone shooting from the camera** in your dream, this shows you are living in your past and you made a collection of the past memories in your head.
- If you see **someone secretly taking pictures** of you in your dreams, this shows some is stalking you or watching your actions in waking life. Like keeping an eye on you for any purpose.

Computer/Laptop

- If you **see a laptop or computer** in your dreams, this is a desire for more technical integration. You want to be more technically advanced.

- If you see **using a laptop or computer** in your dreams, this shows you are working on being more technically advanced in waking life.

- If you see a **cracked laptop** in your dreams, this shows that not being technically advanced shows you as a weak personality in front of people.

Mobile/iPad/telephone

- If you see a **mobile phone lying somewhere**, in your dreams, it shows your intuition or inner voices.

- If you see **yourself using a mobile phone** in your dreams, this shows you are listening to your inner voices.

- If you see a **cracked mobile phone** in your dreams, this shows you are not able to listen your inner voice or not believing your intuition.

Radio

- If you see **yourself listening to radio** in your dreams, this shows that you need to pay attention to the news or messages communicated to you recently.

- If you see a **radio not working** in your dreams, this means you are ignoring the messages that you are receiving in your waking life.
- If you see **becoming a radio jockey** in your dreams, this shows you want to guide people through your words in waking life.

Speakers

- If you see yourself **listening to songs** or others things in your dream, this shows trigger of some powerful past experience in your mind in waking life.
- If you see **your own voice** coming through a speaker in your dream, this means your brain has analysed something about your situation and is trying to guide you.
- If you see a **speaker not working** in your dream, this means you haven't learnt anything from your past experiences and might be still doing the same mistake in waking life.

Television

- If you see yourself **watching a TV** in your dreams, this shows your curiosity or you want to be entertained in real life.
- If you see **yourself on the TV** in any program, in your dreams, this shows your deep connection and

- intentions to be connected to others and share some information with them in waking life.
- If you see a **cracked television screen** in your dreams, this means you are not able to maintain a connection with people or you might be getting betrayal in real life.

- If you see **yourself watching news** in your dreams, this shows you want to aware about your surroundings in waking life.

Watch

- If you see **buying a watch** in your dream, this shows you are hoping that your time will change in your waking life. Expecting some good days in life.

- If you **see time in the watch** in your dreams, this means you are kind of feeling stagnant in life and really wants to progress and move ahead in life.

Other electronic item

- If you see **fire coming out of any of the electronic item,** in your dream, it's the need for change your current life as something (not electronics) is not working in real life.

- If you **see a blast of an electronic item** in your dream, this shows any situation has gone bad or something is dead or ended in your waking life.
- If you **see yourself using any other electronic item** in your dream, this shows your personal transformation.
- If you **experience a shock from any electronic or wire** in your dreams, this shows a personal change, it shows that something inside you is poking you and forcefully making a change happened.

Wedding essentials

Bridal dress

- If you see **wearing a bridal dress** in your dream, this shows your desire for commitment in waking life.
- If you see **a bridal dress** in your dream, this shows new unions or new beginnings in waking life.
- If you see yourself **buying a wedding dress** for yourself in your dreams, it means you are ready for real commitment and relationship in waking life.

- If you see **yourself buying a wedding dress for someone else** in your dreams, it simply means you are happy for someone in waking life. It could be for any achievement that they made in their life.

Wedding ring

- If you see **yourself wearing a wedding ring** in your dreams, this shows deeper commitment in your relations or in career in waking life.
- If you see **wedding ring being stolen** in your dreams, this shows your mind wanders and you are not able to commit to a single thing or relation in your life.
- If you just **see a wedding ring in your dream**, this means a deeper commitment is coming into your waking life.

Priest

- If you see a **priest in your dreams**, this shows spiritual growth in your waking life.
- If you see a **priest chanting mantras** in your dreams, this shows you are looking for peace in waking life.

Wedding hall

- If you see a **wedding hall** in your dreams, this shows you are getting rid of all troubles and worries in your waking life.
- If you see a **wedding hall being turned down** in your dream, this shows you are still facing troubles in waking life.

Wedding decorations

If you see a wedding decoration in your dream, this shows you are about to host any celebration in your life.

Accountant

- If you see **becoming an accountant** in your dream, this means you want to keep the track of your finances in waking life.
- If you see **not able to become an accountant** in your dream, this means you aren't able to keep the track of your finances in waking life.

- If you see **yourself visiting an accountant** in your dream, this means you need someone to keep the track of your finances in waking life.

Astrologer

- If you see **becoming an astrologer** in your dream, you want to manifest a great future for yourself.

- If you see **not able to become an astrologer** in your dream, this means you aren't able to manifest anything in your life right now.
- If you **see yourself visiting an astrologer** in your dream, this means you need guidance on how to take things forward in your waking life.

Actor/actress

- If you see **becoming an actor in your dream**, this shows your innermost desire to get public recognition or fame for your hard work in waking life.
- If you see **not able to become an actor** in your dream, this means you are not getting the recognition or doesn't want a recognition for your hard work in waking life.
- If you see **yourself meeting an actor** in your dream, this shows you are admiring someone's fame in waking life.

Author

- If you see **becoming an author** in your dream, this shows you need to meet people and explore another side of your life. Learning is required.
- If you see that **you are not able to become an author** in your dream, this means that your learning in waking life is going fine.

- If you see yourself **visiting or talking to an author** in your dream, this means you are in crossroads and not able to understand what is required in your life at the moment.

Builder

- If you see **becoming a builder** in your dream, this shows you want to be the designer of your own life and don't want others to dominate you.
- If you see **not able to become** a builder in your dream, this shows that others are trying to dominate you, and you are following the instructions whether you want it or no.
- If you see **yourself visiting a builder** in your dream, this means there is a need or awakening inside to take charge of your own life in your own hands.

Broker

- If you see **becoming a broker in your dream**, this means you know what is best for someone you care about in waking life.
- If you see **not able to broker a news anchor** in your dream, this means you actually don't know how the other person should take things forward in waking life. So don't guide people at this time.
- If you see **yourself visiting a broker** in your dream, this means you are looking for a correct advice in waking life.

Begger

- If you see **becoming a Begger** in your dream, this shows you have loyal and supportive friends in waking life.
- If you see **not able to become a Begger** in your dream, this shows your friends might cheat you in waking life.
- If you see **yourself visiting/meeting or searching a Begger** in your dream, it means you are looking for supportive friends in waking life.

Banker

- If you see **becoming a banker** in your dream, this means you are taking charge of your finances in waking life.
- If you **see not able to become a banker** in your dream, this means you aren't able to take charge of your finances in waking life.
- If you see **yourself visiting a banker** in your dream, this means you are making plans and ideas related to how to handle your finances in waking life.

Chemist

- If you see **becoming a chemist** in your dream, this shows upcoming health concerns in waking life.
- If you see **yourself visiting a chemist** in your dream, this shows you need to get your health checkups done in waking life and some health issue is indicated.

CEO

- If you see **becoming a CEO** in your dream, this shows that you will have to take some very important decisions in your waking life.
- If you see **not able to become a CEO** in your dream, this shows that you aren't able to take some very important decisions in your waking life.
- If you see **yourself visiting a CEO** in your dream, this shows that you desire to take some very important decisions in your waking life.

Doctor

- If you **see becoming a doctor** in your dream, this shows you may suffer setbacks or get dismissed in career, or take a knock in business in waking life.

- If you see **not able to become a doctor** in your dream, this shows you are able to avoid some issues cropping up in your career in waking life.
- If you see **yourself visiting a doctor** in your dream, it represents healing both physically and mentally in waking life.

Driver

- If you see **becoming a driver** in your dream, this shows you are about to change your life for better or worse will depends on your action but a change is certain.
- If you see **not able to become a driver** in your dream, that means your life will go as it the way it was going.
- If you **see yourself visiting or meeting a driver** in your dream, this shows you are looking for an opportunity to change your life for better.

Engineer

- If you see **becoming an engineer** in your dream, it suggests that you have a natural inclination towards problem-solving in waking life.
- If you see **not able to become an engineer** in your dream, this shows you are always confused and not able to solve the issues of your current life.
- If you see **yourself visiting an engineer** in your dream, this shows you are looking for someone who can solve your problems.

Entrepreneur

- If you see **becoming an entrepreneur** in your dream, this shows you need a new beginning in waking life like the way you want it.

- If you see **not able to become an entrepreneur** in your dream, this means you aren't able to design your own life like the way you want it.
- If you see **yourself visiting an entrepreneur** in your dream, this shows the desire to change your life as per your own will.

Fashion designer

- If you see **becoming a fashion designer** in your dream, this shows you are exploring a new way of presenting who you are in waking life.
- If you see **not able to become a fashion designer** in your dream, then you are not able to change the way people perceive you in waking life.
- If you see yourself **visiting a fashion designer** in your dream, this shows you are conscious about your image like how people perceive you in waking in life.

Guide

- If you see **becoming a guide** in your dream, that means you can empathise with people in real life and wants to improve them by telling them where they are wrong.
- If you see **not able to become a guide** in your dream, this means you can empathise with people but do nothing about it in waking life.
- If you see **yourself visiting a guide** in your dream, this means you are looking for someone who can understand you.

Gambler

- If you see **becoming a Gambler** in your dream, this shows you are ready to take risk in your waking life
- If you **see not able to become a habitual gambler** in your dream, this shows you are avoiding risk in waking life.

Gangster

- If you see **becoming a gangster** in your dream, this shows you have a lot of power and independence in waking life and you deal with things aggressively in waking life.
- If you see **not able to become a gangster** in your dream, this shows you have the intention to deal with your situations but doesn't have the power or courage.
- If you see **yourself chased by a gangster** in your dream, this means your inner self is poking you to take the charge of your situation in waking life.

Government/parliament/government employee

- If you see becoming or meeting anyone from government heads or employees or politics then it shows period of uncertainty in your waking life. Some issues will soon crop up related to your career.

Homemaker

- If you see **becoming a homemaker** in your dream, this shows that no one is appreciating your work in waking life.
- If you see **not able to become a home maker** in your dream, this shows you are working very hard and have the desire that people will appreciate your efforts.
- If you **see yourself visiting a home maker** in your dream, this shows you want to be appreciated in real life.

Healer

- If you **see becoming a healer** in your dream, this shows you need physical or emotional healing in waking life.
- If you **see yourself visiting a healer** in your dream, this shows your desire for physical or emotional healing in waking life.

Interior decorator

- If you see **becoming an interior decorator** in your dream, this shows you have the ability of building something new from scratch, and property investment is around the corner in waking life.

- If you see **not able to become an interior decorator** in your dream, this shows you don't have the ability or courage to start anything from the scratch.
- If you see **yourself visiting an interior decorator** in your dream, this shows you are seeking help and guidance from someone who can help you to redesign your life.

IAS officer

- If you see yourself **becoming IAS Officer** in your dreams, this shows you want authority and power in your waking life.
- If you **see yourself not able to become IAS officer** in your dream, this shows you don't get that power in your waking life.
- If you see **yourself meeting/talking or chased** by IAS officer in your dream, this means you are looking for some help and anyone powerful in waking life can only help you in a particular situation.

Investment professional (IP- shares, mutual funds etc)

- If you see **becoming an IP in your dream**, this shows you have gained some wealth recently and you are afraid to lose your wealth.
- If you see **not able to become an IP** in your dream, this means you aren't able to earn the wealth in your life.

- If you see **yourself visiting an IP** in your dream, this means you need tips and ideas to protect your wealth in waking life.

Journalist

- If you see **becoming a journalist** in your dream, this shows you are interested in people and value the lessons that you receive each day in waking life.
- If you see **not able to become a journalist** in your dream, this means you are not able to learn your lessons in waking life.
- If you see yourself **visiting/ chased a journalist** in your dream, this means you are trying to analyse the situation in waking life.

Judge

- If you **see becoming a judge** in your dream, it's time to move your life forward and you are looking for fairness and justice in waking life.
- If you see **not able to become a judge** in your dream, this means you are going fine in your life and doesn't feel the need for fairness and justice in your waking life.
- If you see **yourself visiting a judge** in your dream, this means you need advice in real life about something not going right in your life.

Killer

- If you see **becoming a killer** in your dream, this means you wish to change something in your life in a very drastic way.
- If you see **not able to become a killer** in your dream, this means you aren't able to wish to change something in your life in a very drastic way.
- If you see **yourself visiting/ chased by a killer** in your dream, this means your subconscious is poking you to change something in your life.

Lawyer

- If you see **becoming a lawyer** in your dream, this shows upcoming legal matters or your need to seek guidance in waking life.
- If you see **not able to become a lawyer** in your dream, this shows that you are able to avoid any legal issue in waking life.
- If you see **yourself visiting a lawyer outside lawyer chambers** in your dream, these means you are looking for some advice in your waking life.

Maid

- If you see **becoming a maid** in your dream, this means you are suffering from lack of confidence in waking life.

- If you see **not able to become a maid** in your dream, this means you are confused about things but somehow has the confidence to take things forward once you decide on anything.

- If you see **yourself visiting/meeting or searching a maid** in your dream, this means someone is trying to break your confidence in waking life.

News anchor

- If you see **becoming a news anchor** in your dream, this will bring some unpleasant news in waking life.
- If you see **not able to become a news anchor** in your dream, this shows that you are trying to avoid somethings that you know is unpleasant in waking life.
- If you see **yourself visiting or watching or meeting a news anchor** in your dream, this shows you have a fear of getting an unpleasant news in waking life.

Nurse

- If you see **becoming a nurse** in your dream, this means you have the power to heal or nurture anyone in waking life.

- If you **see not able to become a nurse** in your dream, this means you are not able to heal your closed ones who are suffering in their life.
- If you **see yourself visiting or talking to a nurse** in your dream, this means you are looking for some healing in your life.

Postman

- If you see **becoming a Postman** in your dream, this shows there is a channel of communication opening between or your conscious and subconscious mind.
- If you see **not able to become a postman** in your dream, this shows there is a blockage in channel of communication between or your conscious and subconscious mind. You need to be more spiritually inclined.
- If you see **yourself visiting a postman** in your dream, this means you are looking for answers that what your soul actually wants.

Police/commissioner

- If you see yourself **becoming police** in your dreams, you crave for truth and authority in your waking life.
- If you see yourself **not able to become police** in your dream, this shows you are far away for getting to know the truth or authority in your life.
- If you see **yourself meeting/talking or chased by police** in your dream, this shows feeling of guilt or some fear in waking life.

Radio jockey

- If you see **becoming a radio jockey** in your dream, you need to feel more in tune with your instincts in waking life.
- If you **see not able to become a radio jockey** in your dream, this shows you are guiding other based on your instincts.
- If you see **yourself visiting a radio jockey** in your dream, this means you are analysing the situation with in.

Soldier

- If you see **becoming a soldier** in your dream, this shows you are acting too defensively in some life situation.
- If you see **sacrificing your life** for the country in your dream, this shows you aren't able to defend yourself in some life situation.
- If you are **meeting a soldier** in your dream, this shows your inner self is telling you to defend yourself in some life situation.

Sweeper

- If you see **becoming a sweeper** in your dream, this means you want to clean any negativity in any part of your life.

- If you see **not able to become a sweeper** in your dream, this means you are not able to clean the negativity in your situations in waking life.
- If you see **yourself meeting or talking to a sweeper** in your dream, this means you are looking for someone who can help you in your situations in waking life.

Teacher/profession

- If you see **becoming a teacher in your dream**, this may evoke the feeling of guidance and authority in your life.
- If you see **not able to become a teacher** in your dream, that means you don't feel like guiding anyone in waking life at the moment.
- If you see **yourself visiting a teacher/professor** in your dream, that means you want to understand the whole situation in a better way that's why you are seeking guidance.

Travel agent

- If you see **becoming a travel agent** in your dream, this shows you want to help people in exploring different areas of their life.
- If you see **not able to become a travel agent** in your dream, that even if anyone ask, you are not able to provide any help to anyone.
- If you see **yourself visiting or talking to a travel agent** in your dream, that means you want to alter your life for better.

Thief

- If you see **becoming a thief** in your dream, this shows you have a fear of losing your love, land or reputation in waking life.

- If you see, **not able to become a thief** in your dream, this means you are feeling secure about your possessions in waking life.
- If you see **yourself visiting/chased by a thief** in your dream, you are developing a feeling of insecurity about your possessions in waking life.

Waiter

- If you see **becoming a waiter** in your dream, you are becoming a helpful person or influence in someone's life.
- If you see **not able to become a waiter** in your dream, you aren't becoming a helpful person or influence in someone's life.
- If you see **yourself visiting or talking to a waiter** in your dream, that means you are looking for that helpful influence in your own life.

Superhero's

- If you **see a superhero** in your dreams, this shows your desire to control and ability to overcome obstacles in waking life.
- If you **become a superhero** in your dreams, this means you gain the power to overcome any obstacles in your waking life.

Cartoons

- If you **see any cartoon character** in your dreams, this shows your desire to escape from reality and responsibility.
- If you **become a cartoon character** in your dreams, this shows that you are running from your responsibilities in waking life.

Dolls/Doll house

- If you **see a doll or doll house** in your dreams, this resembles your childhood memories and need to be a child again in waking life.
- If you **become a doll in your dreams**, this shows your innocence and playfulness in waking life.

Barbie/ken

- If you see a **barbie/ken in your dreams**, this shows your need for validation for your physical appearance or beauty in waking life.
- If you **become a barbie/ken** in your dreams, this means you feel that you are perfect when it comes to beauty standards in waking life.

Robots

- If you **see a robot in your dreams**, this shows your lack of emotions and detachment from your surroundings in waking life.
- If you **become a robot in your dreams**, that you have become emotionally unavailable for people in your life.

Past event

If you see exactly the same incident that happened sometime back in waking life, this means you aren't able to forgot the old incident and still feels its negativity in waking life.

Independence era

If you see exactly yourself in an independence era in your dreams, this means you are listening to your own inner voice and exploring your unique expressions.

(Very rarely it will be connected to your past birth. it can be said that's its connected to your past birth only if its recurring since your childhood)

Mughal era

If you see yourself in Mughal era in your dreams, this shows you are looking for authority in your life.

(Very rarely it will be connected to your past birth. it can be said that's its connected to your past birth only if its recurring since your childhood)

Any other civilisation

If you see yourself in any other civilisation in your dreams, this could mean you are about to discover something new in your life.

Ancient temples or Ancient Spiritual places

- If you see visiting an ancient temple in dreams, this means this shows or resembles the lost part of yourself or a forgotten responsibility in waking life. You need to focus, understand and fulfil that responsibility.

King

- If you **see a king** in your dream, this represents issues related to father or husband in waking life.
- If you **see yourself becoming a king** in your dream, this shows you have the desire to rule.

Queen

- If you **see a queen** in your dream, this represents power, authority and control in waking life.
- If you **see becoming a queen** in your dream, this shows that you crave for that power and authority and wants to live your life as per your own wishes.

Names or Alphabets

Alphabets

If you see random alphabets in your dreams, it could resemble a person or animal depends on the alphabet you see. Suppose you see a "d" this could be person whose name starts with d in your life or an animal whose name starts with D like Dog.

Names

- If you see the name **of someone close to you** written in your dreams, this shows you have an unresolved issue with this person whose name you have seen in your dreams, sort things out.
- If you see a **strange name in your dream**, name of someone you don't know in waking life, this shows a spiritual awakening as your guardian angels is trying to connect to you.

- If you **don't able to recall the person's name** in your dreams, this shows you may meet some new people in your life or get connected with old friends again in your life.
- If in your dream **you don't see any name** but hear a name, this shows you have hurt someone and you need to sort things with the person otherwise it will be going to affect your life.

Amusement Park

If you see an amusement park in dreams shows your childish spirit in life.

Autographs

- If you see yourself **giving autograph** to people in your dreams, this shows you will make a quick profit in your waking life.
- If you see yourself **taking autograph** of people in your dreams, this shows you might lose your money in waking life.

Baggage

If you see a heavy baggage on your body or near you in your dream, then it means that you are feeling heavy on your emotions in real life too.

Book store/library

If you see a bookstore or visiting a book store in dreams, this dream is connected to your personal growth and expansion of knowledge in waking life.

Balloons

If you see balloons in dreams, this evoke feeling of happiness and freedom in your waking lives.

Chocolates

If you see chocolates in dreams, this shows feeling of passion and pleasure in waking life.

Camera

If you see camera in dreams, this shows you want to capture some memories in waking life.

Callender

If you see Callender in dreams, this shows that you are going through some phase in life that you need to measure or analyse.

Contract

- If you **see yourself signing a contract** in your dreams, this means someone is dominating you in your life which you really not liking it.
- If you see **not able to sign the contact** in your dream, this shows that you are retaliating with someone dominance in your life.

Fan

If you see a fan moving in your dreams, this shows new Suprises you will receive in your waking life.

Fruits and vegetables

If you see fruits or vegetables in your dreams, it shows good health, good life vitality and abundance in any area of your life.

Gemstones

If you see a gemstone in your dreams, this shows happy situations in your love or career life.

Geometrical shapes

If you see geometrical shapes in your dreams, this means life is taking another shape in waking life. You will encounter changes and its good or bad that time will unfold but change will be there.

Glass

- If you see a **glass in your drea**m, this shows disappointments in waking life.
- If you see **breaking of a glass or broken glass**, it shows you will face major disappointments in your love life or relationships

Gunfire

If you see a gunfire or hear a gunfire in your dream, this represents violence, aggression, anger in waking life.

Joker

If you see joker in dreams, this shows excitement and unpredictability in your waking life.

Kite

- If you see **a kite in your dream**, it means you are hopeful in the situation that you are facing in waking life.
- If you see yourself **flying a kite** in your dream, this shows that you are making efforts towards the situation in your waking life that you are facing.

Kidnapping

- If you see a kidnapping happening in your dreams, (yours or anyone else's) by a stranger, this shows you are getting weak or vulnerable in waking life.
- If you see a kidnapping happening in your dreams, (yours or anyone else's) by someone you know, this means you got hurt by someone very close in your waking life.

Letter

- If you see **receiving a letter** in your dreams, this shows that you are about to receive a wonderful opportunity from the universe in the area you are looking for in waking life.

- If you see **sending a letter** in your dreams, this mean you are giving an opportunity or giving someone a chance to rectify their mistakes in waking life.

Lies

- If you see **someone is telling you** a lie in your dreams, this shows troubles in relationship because of others in waking life.
- If you **yourself telling a lie to someone** in your dreams, this shows trouble in relationship because of your own self.

Magic

If you see a magic in your dream or magic show in your dream, this means you are attracting pleasant surprises in your life.

Mask

If you see yourself or someone else wearing a mask in your dream, it means something is hidden and that could be negative once it's out in public.

Milk

If you see milk, anyone or yourself drinking milk in the dream, this shows that your path will be tough but the end result will be favourable.

Mustache

If you see a Mustache in dreams, it indicates that you aren't happy in your current relationship.

National Flag

If you see a national flag in dream, this shows feeling of patriotism in waking life.

Paintings

If you see a painting in dreams, this shows the intention of making your life perfect or beautifying it.

Petrol

If you see petrol or petrol pump or even smell a petrol in your dreams, it's not a good omen and can lead to disaster in your waking life.

Picnic

If you see yourself or others going on picnic in your dreams, this shows happy times ahead in waking life.

Rejuvenation

If you see any rejuvenation activity like yoga, retreat etc in your dreams, this shows your inner self wants a me time. You need to take some time for yourself.

Random Symbols

If you see any random symbols in your dreams which you can't relate at all, this represents either you need to achieve something in waking life or needs to forget or get over something in waking life.

Rebirth

If you see any dream related to rebirth, this shows new hopes and expectations from life. You are either hopeful or want a new beginning in your life.

Swings

If you see swings or enjoying the swings in dreams, this shows that you are being unstable and you sway a lot in waking life.

Shops or stalls

If you any shops or stalls in dreams, this shows your lack of choices in your waking life. You might have to accept what other told you.

Water Fall

If you see a waterfall in your dream, this means you are able to or already fulfilled your wildest desire in life.

Note:

Any type of dream could be connected to your past births.

Could be anything like ancient places or accidents or becoming a queen. But how to actually identify that if a dream is connected to your past birth.

Very rarely it will be connected to your past birth. it can be said that's its connected to your past birth only if its recurring since your childhood. Yes, dreams connected to past birth will always have a purpose and will be recurring since childhood. The same place and the same feeling again and again.

One needs to focus on the feelings that you get in such dreams like if you are getting feeling of an authority or you want justice or you are looking for some resolvent in some situation.

If it's not recurring then it will be mainly connected to this current birth only.

Sometimes some incident happens that can make us connected to past birth and we actually see that in your youth but always remember dreams that are connected to past birth will always be recurring in nature and always similar feelings that you will experience during the dream.

What is a dream catcher?

It's used as a talisman originated by Ojibwe tribe of north America. It has a wooden structure with a net and decorated with feathers and other items.

What is the purpose of dream catcher?

This is used to protect people esp. children from bad dreams and evil spirit. And to give them peaceful sleep with out any fear or disturbance.

How to use a dream catcher?

Using a dream catcher is very easy. Simply have one dream catcher and hang it in your bedroom esp. near the bed or over your bed or entrance of your bedroom.

Is the use of dream catcher bad?

No, its not bad to use a dream catcher. But as they say dream catcher filter the dreams and send good dreams to you and catches the bad dreams in its net. So, I believe after a while keep on changing your dream catcher or simply every morning put it under the sun for purification.

Can we use dream catcher in cars?

People do hang the dream catcher in car, as the symbol of protection but it will work only for your dreams. So, its best place would be your bedroom.

Accept My Apology

Human mind is the most complicated and complex thing to deal with. The mind could think anything or dream anything.

Humans are emotional beings and they feel a lot of emotions during the day. And whatever they feel, they think about it, any random scenario.

Dreams generate from the thoughts that we put into our subconscious mind.

In this book, I tried to cover as many dreams as I can. But as we all know; human mind is complex so it could see anything in dreams.

So, I apologise to those whose dream are not covered in this book.

Maintain the journal for 5 days.
Write the elements that came in your dreams.

Day1

Element 1:

_____
_____

Element 2:

_____
_____

Element 3:

_____
_____

Element 4:

_____

_____

Element 5:

_____

_____

Element 6:

_____

_____

Element 7:

_____

_____

Element 8:

_____

_____

Element 9:

_____

_____

Element 10:

_____

_____

Write the elements that came in your dreams.

Day 2

Element 1:

_____

_____

Element 2:

_____

_____

Element 3:

_____

_____

Element 4:

_____

_____

Element 5:

_____

_____

Element 6:

_____

_____

Element 7:

_____

_____

Element 8:

_____

_____

Element 9:

_____

_____

Element 10:

_____

_____

Exercise: Your Dream Journal

Write the elements that came in your dreams.

Day 3

Element 1:
_____
_____

Element 2:
_____
_____

Element 3:
_____
_____

Element 4:
_____
_____

Element 5:

Element 6:

Element 7:

Element 8:

Element 9:

Element 10:

Exercise: Your Dream Journal

Write the elements that came in your dreams.

Day 4

Element 1:

Element 2:

Element 3:

Element 4:

Element 5:

_____

_____

Element 6:

_____

_____

Element 7:

_____

_____

Element 8:

_____

_____

Element 9:

_____

_____

Element 10:

_____

_____

Write the elements that came in your dreams.

Day 5

Element 1:

Element 2:

Element 3:

Element 4:

Element 5:

_____

_____

Element 6:

_____

_____

Element 7:

_____

_____

Element 8:

_____

_____

Element 9:

_____

_____

Element 10:

_____

_____

Conclusion

If you have done these exercise for 5 days. You will get to know how to interpret the dream in a better way and can easily remember your dreams now as this exercise can improve your memory and understanding about your dreams.

Improve your thought process to improve your life.

Love

Dr. Purnima Gupta

Other Best sellers from the author:

"The Talking Number" series (Part-1 and Part 2)

Astrology has many forms which can predict our future and numerology or science of number is one such medium by which we can calculate any event in advance. These books are simply the approach of approaching numbers and decoding them to get the answers  of your various questions. This will talk about various numbers that a person gets to see what's working for them and how to deal with the non-working part. Everyone will have a unique combination of numbers that will impact the different areas of a person's life. these books are all about understanding the language of The Talking Numbers. Let's Communicate.

www.ingramcontent.com/pod-product-compliance
Lightning Source LLC
LaVergne TN
LVHW041705070526
838199LV00045B/1214